TRUE IDENTITY

Do you know WHO and WHOSE you really are?

by Jennifer Brommet

ISBN: 978-0-615-79614-7

Library of Congress Control Number: 2013906203

Printed in the United States of America by Booklogix, Alpharetta, Georgia.

This book may be purchased in bulk for educational, business, fundraising or sales promotional use. For information please contact: **Jennifer Brommet, www.trueidentityministries.org**

Cover design by Jennifer Brommet
Cover swan drawing by Jennifer Brommet
Interior layout design by Vanessa Lowry
Editing by Erika Hill and Carina Brommet

All Scripture quotations, unless otherwise indicated, are taken from the *The Holy Bible, English Standard Version*, copyright © 2001 by Crossway Bibles, a division of Good News Publishers. Used by permission. All rights reserved.

Scripture quotations marked NIV are taken from the *Holy Bible, New International Version*. Copyright © 1973, 1978, 1984 by International Bible Society. Used by permission of Zondervan Publishing House. All rights reserved.

Scripture quotations marked AMP are taken from *The Amplified Bible,* Copyright © 1954, 1958, 1962, 1964, 1965, 1987 by the Lockman Foundation. All rights reserved. Used by permission.

Scripture quotations marked KJV are from the King James Version of the Bible.

Scripture quotations marked NASB are taken from the *New American Standard Bible,* Copyright © The Lockman Foundation 1960, 1962, 1963, 1968, 1971, 1972, 1973, 1975, 1977, 1995. Used by permission.

Includes bibliographical references

Dedication

To my loving and supportive family

and to

*My Lord and Savior, Jesus Christ,
who without Him there would be no
True Identity message.
For rescuing me from the dark pit and
setting me free to victorious living!*

Who should we be trying to make the most proud? Our family? Our friends? Our teachers or bosses? What about the one who molded out of the earth itself, who formed up like clay, and instilled within us the very breath of life that shaped the universe?

~ James D. Maxon

Table of Contents

*I have found there are three stages in
every great work of God;
first, it is impossible,
then it is difficult,
then it is done.*

~ Hudson Taylor

Acknowledgements

I couldn't have written this book, or be doing True Identity ministry work, without the love and support of my wonderful husband, Remco. Thank you for being my #1 cheerleader since we first met. Believing in me, encouraging me to step out in faith and share my story, to be confident in who God made me to be, and always telling me I am beautiful and precious to you. For the many times you held down the fort with the girls so I could go and speak, or lead a retreat, develop teaching materials, and write, and launch and lead True Identity Ministries (TIM). For loving me through my cancer journey and giving me hope and determination to keep going for all God had ahead. And recently, for prayerfully developing True Men and helping take the true identity message to men! You have been a Godly husband and father and been such an inspiring example to me of thirsting after an intimate relationship with God. You have modeled prayer and trust, and taken your responsibility as head of our marriage, family, and home with great commitment and care. I love you more and more with each year we share together.

To my precious daughter Carina, you have been an inspiration and great help in the writing and editing of this book. I am so thankful to you. For the many times I dragged you along to help with events for various jobs I've had, and for all the retreats and times I've spoken that you were with me, helped me, and encouraged me, and for the awesome time we shared taking TIM to Kenya! You have had your own amazing journey that I hope someday you will write about. You have been on the True Identity journey yourself and I see God continuing to make you more and more beautiful inside and out. I am so proud of you and all you have pressed through and for your tenacity and determination to stand up for God and what's right in the face of ridicule and loneliness. I love your creativity and the way you see life through a different lens. I can't wait to see what God has planned for this next chapter in your life as you move to London and how He will use all He has put in you and gifted you with for His glory!

To my other precious daughter Sophia, God sent you to our family to bring us great joy! He knew we needed you to lighten us up. You are such a delight and I love your positive outlook on life, your creativity, your passion and care for others, and your wonderful honesty. I love to hear you sing, see you on stage doing what you love to do, and the spiritual maturity and wisdom developing in you. For all those special talks we've had and watching fun videos on YouTube together. I'm excited for you to become more a part of TIM and have opportunities to travel and take the TI message to other places with me. I know God will bring the special plans He has for you to fruition as you continue to walk and trust in Him each step of the way.

To my brothers Les and Larry. You have been on this journey with me my entire life and I thank you for all the years of love, encouragement, and belief in me. It still blows me away every time I speak with you and am reminded of the amazing, redeeming work God has done in our family. We are blessed! Les, I know we had our years of difficulty, but I praise God for how He has redeemed our relationship and given us the opportunity to grow into a special friendship now as adults. You are in inspiration to me as one who has fought some dark battles and pressed through to walk in the light. Your testimony has and will help so many others come to know and trust the Lord! He's just getting started with using you for His kingdom work. Larry, thanks for always being my defender. There were years in school I'm not sure I would have made it without you looking out for me. I thank God He brought you back to an intimate relationship with Him and has launched you out in ministries to help so many others come to know God in a deep and intimate way. It is such a blessing to live near one other and have the opportunity to minister together.

To my dear friend and gifted editor, Erika Hill. You have known me for many years and I remember back when we first knew each other and you told me I should write a book about my story. I've always hoped that when the timing was finally right, you would be the one to help me finish it! You helped give me confidence that I could write this book and have cheered me on each step of the way. Thank you for the years of special friendship, encouragement, and prayers, and now, help in bringing this book to completion. It has been a delight working on this together!

To my True Identity family. What an incredible ride God has had us all on these past five years! You have been an amazing blessing and support to me, encouraging me to write this book, believing that now was the time and helping free me up to get away and write. Thank you for your prayers, wisdom, insight, willingness to give so much of yourselves, and sharing a passion for TIM! I never felt so loved as when I went through my year of oral surgeries and then two years later my cancer treatment. You brought meals, were always there to help, sent gift cards, and lifted my family and I up with powerful prayers! You have been my "Aaron and Hur" standing beside me and holding me up when I grow weary or discouraged. I hope this is just the beginning of many more exciting years God has for us as we continue to take His message of True Identity to His precious daughters and sons all over the world!

To the many friends who have loved me and been such a blessing to me through good times and challenging ones. For the kind words, listening ear, prayers, insight, exhortation, comfort, and help. For the times I wanted to give up and fade away, you helped me to press on and have hope. God has used each of you to be a part of my story, and for that I will be forever grateful.

Introduction
Before You Start This Book

Over the past twenty years, I have been encouraged to write my story and journey to my true identity in Christ. I have been hesitant. "I don't know how to write a book. Others have already written on this topic, and written about it well. I was terrible at spelling and grammar in school, and feel my words can often be a jumbled mess," I said. Then God clearly broke through those lies. He spoke to me and told me that a book could go places I could never go. He wanted this message, HIS message, to get out to His precious daughters, that my story is one that will be of encouragement to others struggling with their identity. He reminded me that He had already given me the foundation for the teaching materials for the True Identity Retreats and events, I had the outline and frame-work, I just needed to flesh it out with stories and compile it into book form. He had inspired men to write the Bible, He could inspire me and give me the words for this book. Someone asked me if I had a ghostwriter. I said, "Yes! The Holy Ghost!" And indeed I did.

Writing this book has been an amazing journey in and of itself! When I was preparing to get away for ten days to begin writing, God told me to bring along my Bible and True Identity teaching notes, the many journals I had saved over the years, and a pad of big white paper with markers. I thought that was a bit strange, but I did.

As I was at my writing retreat destination and ready to get started, I said, "Okay, Lord. Where do I start?" He had me start by going back to the first journal I had from 1977, my second year in college, and read through each and every one, writing down on the pad of paper the things that really stood out. It was not an easy journey to go back through the years of pain and bondage, but as I did, I began to see patterns emerge. I was reminded of the emotions I felt through some very difficult years, as once you are healed and well on the other side of the pain, you do forget some of the feelings. I was overwhelmed with God's grace and mercy and love in my life. He took a broken, shattered soul and put it lovingly back together piece by piece. It was like mapping out my life and seeing God's hand throughout from beginning to now.

I had forgotten that not quite twenty years ago I had written in one of my journals that I had a desire to "help people know what is truth and what is deceptive," and a few years later, while planning a conference, to "talk about our identity in Christ." God showed me that these seeds had been planted much earlier on in my life than I had realized and that He had been weaving this message in me long before we had the first True Identity Retreat. I was blown away! I began to see the "plans the Lord has had for me" (Jeremiah 29:11) laid out on big white sheets of paper. All He allowed me to go through was for this purpose. To share my story, HIS story in me, and be a testimony of the amazing, redeeming work of God. God has written a story in your life, too. Your situations may not be exactly the same as mine were, but we have the same God who is for us and wants to bring all of us to a place of freedom and joy!

This message of True Identity is very prevalent right now. I've heard many pastors speak on this topic, seen it mentioned in books, and listened to talks given on it. Because it is on the heart of so many to share, I truly believe that this is God's message for all of us for "such a time as this!" As the world screams at us to be something we were never designed or intended to be, God's heart is for His sons and daughters to be set free in their TRUE identity in Him.

If you are reading this book alone, I would encourage you to take the time to ponder and pray through the questions at the end of each chapter. Ask yourself each question and take it to God, seeking new insights and understanding through Him. Be open to what He may desire to speak into your life through this book, knowing His ultimate goal is to set you FREE in your TRUE identity in Him so you can have a loving, intimate relationship with Him for eternity.

All quotes at the beginning of each chapter are taken from my journals unless otherwise noted.

My parents.

Chapter 1
Shattered Dreams

I want to be seen for who I am beneath the face.

Life was good for this young couple: a handsome art director with a successful career, and a beautiful former stewardess and model. They loved to socialize with the "in crowd." She was a stay-at-home-mom who enjoyed volunteering for local organizations and their church. She attended regularly, he on holidays and special occasions. They believed in God and doing all the right things to earn their way to heaven.

They had a young son and were building their first house in a quaint Chicago suburb. Their second child was on its way. They were excited to move into their new home and dreamt of life in the suburbs with two perfect children, a dog, friendly neighbors, and a higher social status.

On a cold, blustery December morning in a hospital in northern Illinois, it came time for their second child to be born.

"You have a little girl!" the doctor exclaimed

The mother was thrilled. She got her little girl!

"There is a problem, however," the doctor quietly said.

The mother's heart raced. "What's wrong?" she cried.

"She has a cleft lip and palate."

The mother was in shock. Her world crashed down around her.

"NO! It can't be. This is not happening!" Grief and guilt overwhelmed her.

She opened the blanket and saw a tiny bundle with a perfect body, fingers, toes, soft brown hair, and a terrifying, gaping hole in her face. She'd given birth to a monster.

She started to cry, her heart broken.

"Do you have a name for her?" the doctor asked.

"Yes. Jennifer," the mother stated numbly through her tears.

"I will tell your husband he has a little girl," the doctor said as he walked out of the room.

The doctor smiled weakly, and told the husband that his wife was doing fine, but his daughter had a cleft lip and palate.

The husband stared blankly at the doctor. "No, that can't be," he said. "How can that be?"

The doctor led him into the room. He saw his wife, exhausted and grief stricken, lying on the bed. The baby was not in the room. He went to his wife's side and took her hand.

How could this have happened to them? What did they do to deserve this? How in the world were they going to deal with this? His perfect world had been shattered.

The nurse then brought the baby into the room.

He was not sure he wanted to see her. He'd heard about kids with this issue. They looked like freaks. Not princesses.

The nurse began to hand the baby to him, but he took a step back and shook his head no. She handed the baby to her mother instead.

He slowly stepped toward the bed, glanced at the baby and was repulsed. He was longing to hold her, but couldn't, wouldn't. He was in denial.

"Please, don't take any pictures of her," he said.

Different

My parents rarely spoke of the day I was born, and when they did, they said, "We almost lost you and your mom," or "We don't know why you were born with this deformity," brief answers laced with guilt and shame. It was like some big dark secret that they never wanted to talk about, hanging over most of my life like a mysterious shadow. And indeed, there are no pictures of me until I was about six months old and had had some initial corrective surgery.

Being born with this condition brought with it all kinds of physical challenges. Because of an opening in the roof of my mouth, it was difficult for me to eat, suck, or drink without liquid coming up and out my nose. It caused breathing difficulties, numerous ear infections, sinus issues, and dental and speech problems.

As I grew and became more aware of life and others around me, I began to notice that I was "different." My parents treated me as a normal child, and the neighborhood kids accepted me because we all grew up together and I was just "Jenny" with a scar and funny voice. But when I started school, things began to change.

My heart was pounding with fear as I walked up to school for the first time, tightly gripping my mother's hand. She told me I would love my kindergarten teacher and that I looked pretty in my new dress. I kept my head down, afraid for the other kids to see my face, and didn't talk for fear of being teased for my lispy, difficult to understand voice. My mother walked me to the classroom and introduced me to the teacher. She seemed very nice and said I could sit up front by her. I was struggling to keep back the tears as my mother let go of my hand and said she'd be back for me in the afternoon. I quickly sat down nervously waiting for the other kids to come into the room, trying not to panic that my mother was not there to protect me.

When it came time for recess I reluctantly went outside, staying at the back of the group and near the school building. Some of the boys started laughing, pointing at me and asking, "What happened to your face? Why do you talk so funny?" The girls stared at me, giggled, called me ugly and ignored me. I started to cry, wanting to escape and run home. A teacher came to my aid and took me back to the classroom. It was not soon enough that my mother came to get me and I begged her not to make me go back the next day.

This was long before homeschooling was an option for families so I had to go back the next day, and all the days throughout my elementary, middle and high school years. School became like a prison. Every day I was teased, laughed at, stared at, bullied, and left out. I began to shrink within myself and think of myself as damaged, unwanted, worthless, and as ugly as the others said.

The Long Reconstructive Road

I also was more aware that I was "different" because of the years of surgeries, dental work, speech therapy, ear infections and health issues. Sometimes I missed weeks of school, which in some ways was a relief. I didn't like all the pain and discomfort from treatments, but didn't mind catching up on homework at home. I felt more accepted in the medical community than I did at school. Doctors, nurses, and dentists did not tease me. They were trying to help me.

The first surgery I remember was when I was seven. My mother first took me to consult with a plastic surgeon, who was friendly and talked through all the details with us. I was too young to understand all of what he was talking about, adding to the sense of anxiety in this frightening new experience. The doctor then led me to a room with a camera and lights and took all kinds of pictures of my face from different angles. Each time the bright flash went off, I felt as though I was being stamped with the words "ugly," "deformed," "damaged." The doctor then looked up my nose and in my mouth, and took a lot of notes. The surgery was scheduled for a few weeks later.

I felt terrified as they wheeled me into the operating room and got me on the surgery table. It was cold and sterile with a huge bright light shining over me and all sorts of machines and ominous looking equipment. One nurse put in an IV while another covered me with a blanket and got instruments ready. A few minutes later a hand covered my mouth with a plastic mask, saying to breathe and count to ten. I was out before I got to three.

The next thing I remember was a nurse saying, "Jennifer, wake up. It's time to wake up now. It's all over." I came out of a thick, black fog, the light slowly breaking through, my head clearing and things coming into focus. Nausea and pain came crashing over me as I became more alert. My face was covered in bandages. It was difficult to breathe and I felt wretched.

There is no lonelier place than a hospital room. Especially for a child. My mother stayed with me as much as she could, but she had to go home in the evenings to take care of my family. I cried a lot and wished so much there was another way out of the torment. I went home seven days later with a big, white bandage on my nose and upper lip announcing to the world that I'd had surgery. I couldn't wait to retreat to the safety of my room.

Two weeks later when the bandages came off, I was hoping for a completely new and normal face to be revealed. What I saw was disappointing. My nose was swollen and didn't look much different and I had a puffy upper lip with lots of stitches. They removed the stitches and said things would look much better in a few more weeks once the swelling went down and the incisions healed. Each morning when I got up and looked in the mirror, I hoped I would see a beautiful, new face. But the reflection was still one of a scarred, crooked nosed little girl, and it was hard to fight off the discouragement and dashed hopes.

Along with surgeries, I spent many years in the dentist and orthodontist chair. I dreaded going to both. I had braces on my baby teeth from age six through eleven, and again when I was twelve through age seventeen. I couldn't remember what it felt like to run my tongue over smooth teeth. To smile and not have metal cutting into my gums and causing sores, or constantly changing rubber bands and wearing head gear at night. Many times I wished the doctor would just pull all my teeth out and give me fake ones. In spite of the long and painful process, I continued to cling to the hope that all the treatment would some day help me look "normal" and bring an end to the teasing and rejection.

Creative Escape

My mother, the gorgeous former model and airline stewardess, always did her best to make me feel pretty. She bought me cute outfits and tried to make my hair look nice. She thought I looked best with short permed hair, while I wanted long flowing hair like all my friends. "You look like a boy" was added to the slurs hurled against me at school. There were many days I wished paper bags were in fashion so I could wear one over my head. My mother often told me I had beautiful eyes and elegant hands, or that I was a good artist, or had a wonderful personality, hoping to encourage me and draw me out of my unhappiness. I so longed to be pretty like her. Everyone liked her.

My father was kind to me, but always a bit distant. He was protective of me and I know he loved me but he had great difficulty showing it. I always felt like I didn't quite measure up and that he thought girls were only worthy if they were beautiful.

My mother encouraged me to take ballet because it made me feel graceful and princess-like, and when I was dancing I could lose myself in a fairy tale world. I took dance lessons for eight years, but I was never chosen for any lead parts. When I tried out for a jazz dance ensemble in high school I was passed over for the "cute" girls. Later, they would come and ask me if I could help them choreograph their dances for them, driving the knife further in and twisting it.

My other escape was drawing. It started at age seven when my parents gave me a Barbie light box and drawing kit for Christmas. I would use the light box to trace and draw all kinds of different outfits on Barbie. I loved it and pretended I was her. Perfect and pretty.

Move

All through my adolescent years, the message that I was "different and ugly" was reinforced. In the summer of my ninth year, we moved from the North Chicago area to a smaller town in the middle of Wisconsin, and I was surrounded by a new group of tormentors. The constant question of, "What happened to your face?" persisted and because I still had a small opening in the roof of my mouth and had difficulty pronouncing words, I was repeatedly asked, "What did you say?"

One afternoon a week, for seven years, I went and spent an hour with the school speech therapist. When I was excused from class to go, kids would laugh and make comments about how "the freak was going to learn how to talk." The therapists worked with me to develop clearer pronunciation, to use my mouth differently to form the words I struggled with. It didn't seem to change much for me. I still spoke with a lisp and kids still relentlessly asked me what I was saying. I grew more and more self-conscious when I talked, and by the time I was twelve I had stopped talking unless it was necessary. Instead, I spent a lot of time by myself in my room, where it was safe, studying or drawing, but I was alone and lonely.

Trapped

By middle school and high school I was the "ugly sister," sandwiched between two good-looking brothers whom everyone liked. My older brother teased and taunted me along with all his friends while my younger brother was my defender.

One summer afternoon I was home alone and all of sudden I heard banging on the back door. I went to look out and it was the neighbor boy. He started yelling, "Hey, ugly girl, I'm going to come in there and get you!" I was terrified and locked the door. Then he, and my older brother, who had joined in, were pounding on the door of the porch, both laughing and yelling, "We're coming in to get you!" I quickly ran and locked that door. In a panic I also locked all the other doors in the house. Soon there were other boys with them banging on different doors all around the house, shouting and taunting me. I ran up to my room, locked my door, and buried myself in a blanket, crying and shivering in fear. Eventually they stopped and went off to play at the neighbor's house. Even though my parents reprimanded my brother, from that day on I lived with the constant worry that my brother and his friends would attack me when I least expected it. Because of this, I avoided my brother as much as possible and barely spoke to him.

On the flip side, my younger brother was always willing to stand up to those who would tease or bully me. Since we were just one year apart in school, he would often walk with me to my locker and sometimes to my first class. He would check-in at lunch and see how I was doing and was positive and loving toward me. I always felt secure with him.

However, being surrounded by a good-looking, well-liked family always made me feel like an embarrassment, driving me to become more and more withdrawn. I immersed myself further in drawing and discovered a love for photography. They were both safe and fun, because I could be creative and do them alone.

Before You Read On

1. Do you have a shattered dream? How does it make you feel?

2. Have you ever felt different than others?

3. How do you escape hurt or stress in your life?

SUGGESTED PRAYER

Heavenly Father, You know my shattered dreams. You know how life can come crashing down and bring great disappointments. You know of the times when I may feel different or don't feel like I fit in. Help me to turn to You and look for healthy escapes and stress relievers when life feels hurtful and unfair. Give me faith to believe that You will bring me the deepest comfort and peace in the midst of life's fiery trials. In Jesus' name ~ Amen.

First photo of me around 6 months old.

With my favorite doll around age 3.

Chapter 2
Why Me?

*All the operations and encouragement just don't
make up for all the put downs and rejection.
I don't understand the purpose in this?*

By the time I was fifteen, I had had numerous corrective surgeries and extensive dental work, all very difficult and painful. After a surgery the summer of my fifteenth year, I sat staring at myself in the mirror. The bandages would come off in a week. What would lie underneath? Would I be disappointed like I had so many times before? The doctors said they took the bump out of my nose, moved the septum over so I could breathe better, and made the tip a little smaller, along with refining the scar above my lip. But all I saw was a big white bandage on my nose, ugly black stitches above my swollen upper lip, and two black eyes. Every breath was a struggle and I was trying desperately not to cry. I hurt, outside and inside, and I still wondered if all these surgeries and years of dental work would actually make me look normal. Forget pretty. I would be happy with normal.

"Why me?" I would often ask. "Why must I be sentenced to this curse my whole life? What did I do to deserve this?

It's so unfair!" I was slowly spiraling down into a place of deep depression. I was in the bottom of a dark, slimy pit, with no light and no way to get out. I'd lost all hope that anything would change or get better. I hated myself and my life.

I spent many nights crying myself to sleep and began to feel that everyone would be better off without me around. My parents wouldn't have to keep paying for medical bills, my father wouldn't be disappointed, and my brothers wouldn't be embarrassed or have to defend me. I started thinking of the easiest and most pain-free way to end my life.

This Is It

One night in my sixteenth year, my parents were at one of their many weekend parties, and my brothers were out with friends. I thought, "This is it. I'm doing it tonight." I got some liquor, amply supplied in our house, and some Tylenol PM. Just when I was ready to take them and drink some alcohol, my older brother came home unexpectedly. I panicked and hid the pills and the bottle under my bed. He knocked on my door and asked what I'd been doing. I started sobbing, saying I didn't want to live anymore. I was sick of all the teasing and pain and knew everyone would be better off without me around. He had no idea what he had interrupted or how to handle my crying and said, "Jenny, why are you making such a big deal of all this? It's just a little scar." I looked at him in disbelief. The brother who was always taunting and teasing me and getting his friends to join in was dismissing my pain? Now I was mad. I screamed at him to get out. Unsure of what to do, he called my parents and told them I was falling apart and they needed to come home.

About an hour later, my parents arrived, somewhat intoxicated and perturbed that I had interrupted their party. However, it was a wake up call for my family. My mom tried even harder after that, buying me nice clothes, giving me new art supplies, anything to pacify me. My older brother was a bit kinder and my younger brother increased his role as my protector. But my dad just kept himself detached and immersed in his work, and nothing anyone did or said made me feel better. I longed for people to see the "real" me. The Jenny behind the marred face. Except I was certain I was doomed to be "the ugly one" and rejected the rest of my life.

Summer Camp

I grew up attending church regularly. I knew all the hymns and Bible stories, knew about God and Jesus, and had been confirmed in the church. But I believed that God didn't love me and wasn't interested in me, was even punishing me. However, I also thought if I followed the rules I could go to heaven when I died. So I just went through all the motions at church and did what was expected of me.

The summer I was sixteen, my mother wanted to send me to church camp, hoping it would be a positive and fun experience for me. For me, though, going and spending a week away from home with a group of strangers hardly sounded fun, and my younger brother wouldn't be there to defend me. But I reluctantly went.

A group of kids I would call "Jesus Freaks" were there. I watched them from afar, thinking they were crazy. But they didn't make fun of me. They talked to me and genuinely seemed interested in me. This intrigued me and I kept thinking, "What's the catch? What do they want from me? No one's ever nice to me." They started telling me God loved me and Jesus wanted to be my friend. Now I really thought they were crazy. How could a loving God allow a child to be born with a defect that causes years of pain and suffering? I kept my distance and endured the rest of the week at camp, glad to return home and retreat to the safety of my room.

My junior year in high school was just as tough as my sophomore year. I still had thoughts of ending my life and found solace in photography, drawing, and now food. I figured since I was already ugly, it didn't matter if I was also fat. I still cried myself to sleep and went through days in the grip of intense depression, still desperately trying to find a way out of that deep, slimy, dark pit.

The summer of my junior year, my mother sent me back to the church camp. She knew she couldn't help me, but perhaps God could.

So off to camp I went again. This time my younger brother went, too, and I felt safer having him with me. Some of the same "Jesus Freaks" were back. "Great... here we go again," I thought. But there was a new guy there, David. He was really nice and handsome and seemed interested in me. Since I'd never had an attractive guy interested in me, I thought I'd listen to what he had to say.

He asked me what I liked to do and eventually how I felt about God. I told him that I believed God didn't love me because He allowed this terrible thing to happen to me. David told me God loved me very much and He let this happen to me for a reason. I might not understand that right now, but someday I would. He said that God had a special plan for my life and wanted me to know how much He loved me and longed to have a relationship with me. I had never heard anyone tell me about a personal relationship with God before. I knew all the Bible stories from going to church. God had a relationship with some of the people in the Bible and the priests, holy people, but not with common people like me.

David spent the week showing me Bible verses that explained how God loved me so much that He sent His son Jesus to die for my sins so I could be reconciled to Him and have a personal relationship with Him. (John 3:16) He asked me why I was so fearful to receive God's love. I told him it was because whenever I let anyone near me I got rejected and hurt. God would surely do the same.

David said he was praying for me and hoped that I would come to a place of understanding and acceptance of God's love. He asked if he could keep in touch after camp was over.

Rescued

Several weeks later, David invited me to join him and some other kids at a lake for a few days. I went, not sure what to expect. I loved being by a lake—I had spent many summers by the lake at a family summer home in Northern Wisconsin—and I was excited to spend a few days with a cute guy.

The first night the group talked about Jesus like He was their best friend and shared about the wonderful things He had been doing in their lives, things I'd never heard before. They told me that they had freedom in His forgiveness, that He spoke to them through reading the Bible, gave them insight and understanding, that God had a plan for their life and was in the details of that plan, and He loved them more than any human ever could or would. They didn't push me or preach at me, just shared their own experiences. I was intrigued and drawn to their sense of joy, peace, and contentment, but I still couldn't figure out why they cared about me.

The next night they asked if I was ready to pray and ask God to forgive my sins, make Jesus Lord of my life, surrender to Him and receive all He had for me. I had done a lot of thinking since I had talked with David at camp. I was already trapped at the bottom of the pit, so what could it hurt? Maybe I could actually have some sort of relationship with God. Perhaps He really did love me and could help me out of the paralyzing grip of depression and hopelessness. If not, I had lost nothing.

So we prayed. I said I believed that Jesus had died for my sins and risen on the third day and now ruled with God in heaven. (Romans 10:9-10) I asked God to forgive me of my sin, be my Lord and Savior. I wanted Him to invade my life and fill me with His Holy Spirit. I wanted to be His and really know He loved me. I wanted to be free and be at peace.

The instant I finished that prayer, I felt as if a huge weight had lifted off my shoulders. My body was flooded with warmth, love, and that deep peace I longed for. This is what they had meant about the love of God filling us!

I cried, laughed, rejoiced, and couldn't stop smiling and hugging everyone. For the first time in my life I truly felt loved.

The next day I was baptized in the lake. I felt the "old" me go under the water and the "new" me come up. (2 Cor. 5:17) Reborn, alive, FREE. As I looked up to the sky I sensed God was smiling down on me. I was overwhelmed with gratitude and I couldn't wait to go home and tell my parents and my brothers. He rescued me from the pit!

New Beginnings

My family could tell I was different. My mom was pleased that I was happier, but my dad and older brother thought I'd gone off the deep end and become a "Holy Roller Jesus Freak." My younger brother wanted to know more, though. He'd been at camp and God had been working in his heart, too.

I told some of the kids at school and word spread like wildfire. "Jenny's a Christian now! Our prayers have been answered!" I thought this was a bit odd since I didn't know any of them were Christians except for one kid whose dad was a pastor. However, they invited me to join a Bible study. I was hungry for the things of God and what He wanted to teach me. Since I had accepted Christ, my eyes and spirit were opened and now when I read the Bible it was as if God was speaking directly to me. Words would jump off the page with a completely new understanding and insight, speaking life and nourishment into my thirsty soul! I was also feeling more accepted and open to risk being friends with others.

Before You Read On

1. How do you see yourself? Write down 10 words that you would use to describe yourself.

2. Are you in a place in your life where you feel you need to be rescued?

3. Do you know how much God loves you? Do you have a personal relationship with Him? If not would you like to pray to do so? Romans 10: 9-10 will give you insight as to what to pray. He is waiting to rescue you and have a special relationship with you!

4. If you do have a personal relationship with Christ, share with someone how God may have rescued you or the time when your faith really became personal and your own.

SUGGESTED PRAYER

Heavenly Father, thank you loving me so much you sent your Son Jesus to pay the penalty for MY sin on the cross. Please forgive me of my sins and for anything that has been standing in the way of me fully receiving your love and surrendering my will to yours. Please come and be Lord of my life. Help me to trust you to bring me to full healing of the hurts and wounds in my life and be a witness for all you have done in my life. Thank you for rescuing me from myself and blessing me with freedom and abundant life in you. In Jesus' name ~ Amen.

My brothers and I ready for a birthday party.

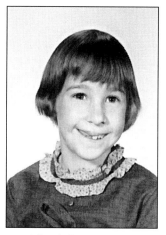

School photo at age 7.

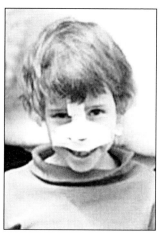

First surgery I remember at age 7.

*School photo at age 8.
I remember having this taken
several times trying to get a
decent picture.*

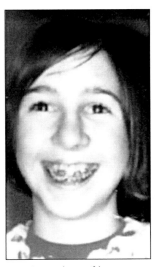

*Second set of braces
at age 13.*

With my Barbie drawing kit at age 9.

High School Graduation 1975. *My beautiful mother.*

Chapter 3
The Ugly Duckling

I'm so tired of feeling ugly.

I graduated high school glad to have those torturous years behind me and ready to move on to college. I was nervous to leave home and live in a dorm with strangers, but overall was looking forward to a change. Also, I didn't know anyone from my high school class who was going to the same college, so I could have a fresh start where no one had any history with me.

Food had become my ally and comfort, and I knew I needed to lose weight. Would I be teased for that, too? Or would they act more like adults and accept me? The excitement of tackling art, design, and photography studies outweighed the apprehension. I also knew there were some Christian groups I could get involved in and surely they would be accepting of me. And, above all else, I knew God was going with me.

The first two years of college were challenging and fulfilling. I loved being able to take classes in subjects I enjoyed and I was beginning to grow out of the "ugly duckling" stage. I lost weight, let my hair grow out, and got my braces off. Guys started paying attention to me, saying I was pretty. I thought they were joking. Couldn't they see the scar, asymmetrical nose, and uneven lip? I wouldn't let any of them get close to me. Instead, I focused on my studies, Bible study, and hanging out with my roommates. I still didn't talk much and people still made comments and stared, but it didn't rock me the way it used to. God was giving me strength and hope that someday things would get better.

When I was twenty-one I had one last surgery to close the small opening in the roof of my mouth and further refine my nose and lip. A nurse showed me how to use special makeup to cover the scar and look more normal. After years of speech therapy, reconstructive surgeries, and dental and orthodontic work, I could talk clearly enough that others could understand me, and I was not quite as self-conscious about my looks. Up until this point my identity had been focused on my physical appearance, and all in a negative way. Everything was colored by perpetual judgment, rejection, and a constant sense of inadequacy from all sectors in my life; my parents, doctors, teachers, friends, society. I felt as if I was let out of a prison!

At this time my mother came to me in tears and said, "You know that Ugly Duckling story? Well that's *your* story." In Hans Christian Anderson's story, *The Ugly Duckling*, a duckling is rejected and considered ugly because he's different from all the other ducks. Later, when he is grown, he sees his reflection in a lake and realizes he's not a duck, he's a beautiful swan.

My mother reminded me that I too was no longer an ugly duckling but a swan, and she handed me a little glass swan. It was the most precious gift my mother ever gave me, and to this day swans have held a very special place in my heart. Not only because they remind me of how God sees me and what He brought me out of, but also of my mother and the special love she had for me. Especially since I lost her four years later to cancer.

Your Story

As creatures living in a sinful, fallen world, we have all experienced rejection or been wounded in some way. Perhaps you have been abused, or come from a broken home, were abandoned, lost something dear to you, were bullied or teased, had a failed relationship, or were told things that deeply wounded your soul. You are not alone.

Like the ugly duckling, we all need to see our reflections from the proper source and discover our true identity. My mother was the first to tell me that I was no longer an ugly duckling, but a swan. Years later, I realized I had always been a swan, but just never knew it. My hope is that my story will encourage you to share yours, and your own journey to healing and freedom can begin.

Come with me on a journey of discovering WHO and WHOSE you truly are!

Before You Read On

1. What type of things has caused you to feel rejected or hurt?

2. How do you usually deal with rejection or hurt?

3. Who in your life is someone you can go to when you are hurting? How do they help you?

4. Everyone has a story. All of mankind has been through difficult, hurtful, wounding experiences. What is your "Ugly Duckling" story? Share your story with a trusted friend or small group. You'll feel better after you do.

SUGGESTED PRAYER

Heavenly Father, thank you that when I feel shattered and broken I can come to you and you understand my deepest pain. Thank you also for others you have placed in my life to comfort and encourage me. Help me, as the Ugly Duckling did, to see myself as you see me. As I begin this journey of discovering my TRUE identity, allow me to trust you with my deepest hurt, knowing that you will bring healing and freedom. In Jesus' name ~ Amen.

At my friend's wedding. Still
battling weight and ugly
duckling issues.

At my brother's wedding
4 years later.

Around age 24.

Chapter 4
Lies, Lies, Lies

I'm feeling worthless and awful about myself.
I know Satan uses this weakness to try to defeat
me and sow great doubts in my mind and heart.

After graduating from the Milwaukee Institute of Art and Design with a BFA in advertising and graphic design, I worked as a graphic designer in the advertising department of Gimbel's Department Store in Milwaukee, Wisconsin. I had recently been "promoted" from housewares ads to lingerie ads and my job was to supervise the lingerie photo shoots.

Before computers and Photoshop, the developed prints from the photo shoot went to the Airbrush Guy. Knowing what the art director wanted, I would tell the Airbrush Guy to trim down the model's thighs, take a few inches off her waist, augment her breasts, and clear up her skin. The finished result looked stunning, but it wasn't what I had seen downstairs in the photo shoot! Now with computers and Photoshop, artists can make even more dramatic changes: lengthen the neck, make eyes bigger or a different color, change the shape of eyebrows or nose, plump up lips, even put someone's head on someone else's body. I often wonder why they even bother using a model. They can create whatever they want and the viewer has no way of knowing what is real.

Marketers use deception to manipulate people's desires and perceptions of acceptance. "Advertising capitalizes on the longing of people for a positive focus in their lives," states Sarah Young in her devotional, *Jesus Calling*. We are convinced that if we look a certain way, have certain things, or have attained a certain level of success and admiration, we will feel fulfilled. At the core of all this is the master of crafting hollow lies.

Day Of Deception

We are bombarded daily with lies and deception, convincing us that we are "ugly ducklings," physically, emotionally, or spiritually distorting our identities and offering empty promises of fulfillment and hope.

Picture this: Your alarm fails and you wake up late, with no time for your usual quiet time with the Lord. "Well, that's okay," you say, "because I'm not sure God really hears my prayers anyway." You shower, using the best products to make your hair shiny and your body clean and smooth. You dry off and look in the mirror, feeling like this is going to be another 'fat and ugly' day. Maybe Mary Kay can help! Your breakfast is a diet drink because if you lose five pounds you can fit into that cute outfit you bought a few weeks ago and you'll feel better about yourself. You turn the news on and see Ken and Barbie describe the terrible events happening in your city and around the world, with perfect smiles on their faces. You fix your family's breakfast and pack their lunches. Your husband rushes out the door without a kiss goodbye. Your kids defy you all morning. All the way to work you feel like an unattractive wife and a bad mother. But you have a great job and are driving there in your new BMW! Once there, you have a productive morning, until your boss tells you that you are being moved to a different office space because they need room for the new guy who's *really* talented. You consider calling a friend for lunch, but decide against it because she has a wonderful job, marriage, and kids, and always looks like she stepped out of a magazine. Seeing her would only make you feel more depressed.

You make it through the rest of your day, stop by the grocery store, and at the checkout stand glance at the magazines. "If I could only look like that, my life would be perfect," you tell yourself with a sigh. You get home, throw dinner together—mostly processed diet foods that say "healthy" on the package to help you lose those five pounds. You turn on the TV to relax with your husband after your grueling and depressing day. You watch for a bit, admiring the nice house the family on the show lives in and wondering if you can get your house to look like that. You begin to think that if your husband had a better job perhaps you could live in a house like that. In fact, you deserve to live in a house like that.

You head upstairs to get ready for bed. You brush your teeth with the latest teeth whitening product and slather anti-aging cream on your face, thinking, "If I can look 10 years younger, everyone will notice me and admire me more." You crawl in bed and read a bit of your romance novel, wishing your life was like that of the heroine in the book and your husband would talk to you and treat you the same way the wonderful, hunky hero treats her. "If only…" is your last thought before you drift off to sleep.

Ever had a day like that?

The CEO Of Deception

1 Peter 5:8, *"Be alert and of sober mind. Your enemy the devil prowls around like a roaring lion looking for someone to devour"* (NIV).

A recent example of Satan's craftiness is a situation I experienced while away with my ministry board and prayer team for a ministry prayer retreat. The first evening of the retreat I received an email from a pastor in England inviting me to be a guest speaker at a women's conference a few months away. They would cover all the expenses for my travel, accommodation, and meals, as well as pay a substantial speaker fee. The pastor encouraged me to visit their church website for more information about their church. The website and church both seemed very legitimate, had an advertisement about the women's conference, and after listening to one of the pastor's sermons, I got very excited about the possibility to go to England and be a part of this conference!

I emailed him with questions to clarify some details. He responded the next day with more information about speaking at the conference, a letter of invitation, contract, and instructions for getting a UK entry visa. He said once I had the UK entry visa, they could make my travel arrangements and send me a speaker fee deposit.

On our way home, the pastor called me, introducing himself asking me if I had received the email and had contacted the border official to secure an entry visa. I told him yes, and he answered a few more of my questions and told me how excited they were. I had a fleeting thought that he did not sound like the pastor in the video on the website, but I assumed it was from a bad phone connection.

That evening as I prayed, the phrase, "Wolf in sheep's clothing" kept coming to mind. The next morning I received an email from the border official asking for some basic information and $600 through Western Union for a *work permit*, not an entry visa. I sensed that something was wrong. My husband and a friend and I looked more closely at the contract, compared information in it with information about the church, and things were not matching up. We questioned, "Since when does the British government work through Western Union? Why does the contract say they will put me up in a hotel in London when the conference is in South Wales? Why did the "pastor" on the phone sound different than the pastor on the church video? Why are they so insistent that I pay $600 for a work permit as a guest speaker at a conference? We decided to email the church directly, at a different email than the "pastor" was using, and inquire if they had indeed invited me to come and speak.

We heard back from the church the next morning. They had not invited me. This was a scam, and they were aware of it and were investigating! Wow! It was a very cunning and well-thought through scam. Satan made it all look so real and good, even using it right on the heels of major spiritual breakthroughs with our prayer retreat.

Satan is an evil, conniving foe, dressed up like a compassionate, caring person who has your best interests at heart. Don't fall for it!

When an army prepares to go into battle, they study their enemy. My father often shared stories of studying the German army and their tactics before his army company would engage in battle during WWII. It is similar with us. As we are living in this world, which is ruled by Satan, the Prince of Darkness, we need to be aware of the enemy and how he operates.

John 8:44 tells us this about Satan; *"he was a murderer from the beginning, and has nothing to do with the truth, because there is no truth in him. When he lies, he speaks out of his own character for he is a liar and the father of lies."*

Satan's character is to lie. He is the *father* of all lies, yet we act like he doesn't exist, or only lies some of the time. We keep giving him a second chance, believing he wants to bring us fulfillment, peace, and joy. However, 2 Thessalonians 2:9 warns us, *"The coming of the lawless one will be in accordance with how Satan works. He will use all sorts of displays of power through signs and wonders that SERVE THE LIE"* (NIV).

Satan's goal is to drive a wedge between us and God, keep us from growing in our relationship with Him, and lead us into strongholds and bondages that will eventually destroy us. Luke 8:12 says, *"Those along the path are the ones who hear, and then the devil comes and takes away the word from their hearts, so that they may not believe and be saved"* (NIV).

His strategy is to convince us that God doesn't exist or if He does, that He doesn't love us, is distant and condemning, cannot help or save us. Since Adam and Eve in the garden, (Genesis 3), Satan has been whispering in our ears that "if only _____, we would be happier, wiser, richer, prettier, like God." That we will find our fulfillment from the WORLD, not in God.

Satan knows exactly how to entice us, give us half-truths and twist scripture just enough for us to take the "bait." It starts with a lie that can come to us via our thoughts, something we hear, or innocent looking situations or objects (books, movies, newspapers, magazines, etc.). 2 Corinthians 11:14 tells us *"Satan disguises himself as an angel of light."*

"It's usually not obvious. It can be disguised as a New York Times Best Seller, popular magazine, movie, TV show, Top Ten hit song. May even pose as a relative or friend giving sincere counsel, a therapist, Christian writer, preacher or counselor. May sound right, feel right, seem right, but if it is contrary to the Word of God, it ISN'T RIGHT!" -Nancy Leigh DeMoss

2 Timothy 2:26 – *"And that they will come to their senses and escape from the trap of the devil, who has taken them captive to do his will"* (NIV).

1 Peter 5:8 – *"Be alert and of sober mind. Your enemy the devil prowls around like a roaring lion looking for someone to devour"* (NIV).

3 Main Channels Of Deception & Temptation

1 John 2: 15-16 states, *"Do not love the world or the things in the world. If anyone loves the world, the love of the Father is not in him. For all that is in the world—the desires of the flesh and the desires of the eyes and pride in possessions—is not from the Father but is from the world."*

And it is not God who tempts us. James 1:13-16 tells us, *"Let no one say when he is tempted, 'I am being tempted by God.' For God cannot be tempted with evil, and he himself tempts no one. But each person is tempted when he is lured and enticed by his own desire. Then desire when it has conceived gives birth to sin, and sin when it is fully-grown brings forth death. Do not be deceived."*

Satan's deception will come through three main channels;

• **Lust of the Flesh** – This deception tells us to fulfill our needs outside the boundaries of God's will.

For example, we need to eat to live, but over-eating is giving in to the lust of the flesh, as is starving ourselves to attain a weight we believe is desirable. We are designed to be in sexual relationship with a spouse, but we give in to sexual desire outside a marriage or become addicted to pornography. This can be said of just about any addiction. We are letting our flesh rule over us instead of living within the loving, boundaries that God set in place to protect us and give us a fulfilled and healthy life in Him.

- **Lust of the Eyes** – This deception causes us to desire what the world has to offer, more than we desire to trust in God's loving provision. We see something (or someone), want it, and think we deserve it. This is the belief that things of the world rather than God will fulfill us and make us happy, and that we deserve to have what we see and want. It makes us selfish, lovers of money, workaholics, shopaholics, determined to "make it big" at any cost, instead of being content and trusting God to provide for our needs. It drives people to covet, lie, steal, cheat, and even kill to have what they believe will bring them fulfillment and happiness. But, Matthew 6:24 – *"No one can serve two masters, for either he will hate the one and love the other, or he will be devoted to the one, and despise the other. You cannot serve God and money."*

- **Pride of Life** – This deception leads us away from worshiping God by urging us to become our own gods. The world loves the self-made man, or rags to riches stories, but often they lift up man and what he has accomplished rather than giving glory to God. They tempt us to say, "Look what I've accomplished. I am better than everyone else. I don't need God. I determine my own destiny."

Pride is ugly and destructive. Proverbs 16:18 reminds us, *"Pride goes before destruction, and a haughty spirit before a fall."* When someone is driven to constantly appear right or better than everyone else it is only a matter of time before he falls. We've seen this happen with ministry leaders, politicians, businessmen, celebrities, and other people with power and influence. They build a kingdom for themselves and then they lie or secret is revealed and their world comes tumbling down. Remember, *"God opposes the proud."* (James 4:6).

Every one of us has areas of vulnerability, and the enemy knows what they are. Be alert!

He will bring the perfect temptation along at your most vulnerable time.

Before You Read On

1. Describe Satan's character in your own words.

2. Where do lies come from?

3. What are the ways in which Satan deceives us and lies to us?

4. What areas are you most vulnerable to temptation and in which situations?

5. How do you usually deal with temptation? Do you resist and flee, or do you give in and justify?

SUGGESTED PRAYER

Dear Heavenly Father, please help me to be alert to Satan's schemes and temptations. Show the ways in which the enemy is trying to tempt and entrap me. Help me to flee temptation instead of giving in and then trying to justify my actions. Take the blinders off my eyes and lead me into your truth. In Jesus' Name ~ Amen

Satan is so much more in earnest than we are—he buys up the opportunity while we are wondering how much it will cost.

~ Amy Wilson-Carmichael

Chapter 5
Smorgasbord of Lies

I stopped reading ladies magazines.
They only fed the lie of
"I'm never quite good enough."

Satan is pretty creative and has a whole smorgasbord of lies that he can throw at us. However, his deception and temptations will often come through the three channels mentioned in the previous chapter, lust of the eyes, lust of the flesh, and pride of life, with these types of lies:

- lies of comparison – false goals

- temptation lies (bait/hook)

- lies of conscience – justify/manage sin

- accusatory, condemning lies – false identity

Lies of Comparison

One of the biggest deceptions for women is being told by the unreal, "Hollywoodized" media that if we don't look young and beautiful, we are not of any value.

LADIES, WE ARE BEING LIED TO! Most everything you see in magazines and in the media has been retouched, which means the standard we are being held against isn't even real! Even the *models* aren't quite beautiful enough. *We are all striving after something that is impossible to achieve.*

This was reinforced for me in the Philippines a few years ago. Driving around Manila, I noticed places for getting your skin lightened and your nose enlarged and straightened. At a women's gathering I asked the Filipina women their idea of beauty. They said, "To look like Americans or Europeans." I told them, "That's funny. In America we all want tanned skin and little noses like YOU!" Beauty comparison is universal. I experienced a similar thing in Kenya. The Kenyan standard of beauty is a dark-skinned, larger woman. They looked at me and thought, "You need to darken your pale skin and put some fat on those bones!" They were always telling me I should eat more, just the opposite of American culture. Each culture has its own standards of beauty, often something different than the norm or unachievable for most people.

I grew up with Barbie dolls and spent most of my childhood longing to look like Barbie and live in the perfect world I had created for her. As I got older it transferred to buying the latest women's magazines to learn the beauty secrets of the stars, trendy new fashion tips, and how to "walk off five pounds in one week." (I never understood why these magazines always had pictures of desserts on the cover with this type of headline underneath. I bet Barbie didn't eat cake.). After a while, I realized this was only feeding the "I'm not quite good enough and don't measure up" lie. So I stopped. Same went for romance novels.

At first it seemed so innocent to escape into the fantasy world described in these books, every woman rescued and swept off her feet by a handsome Prince Charming to live "happily ever after" in a pristine castle or mansion. When I realized it was making me feel very discontent with myself, my family, and my place in life, I knew I had to stop. I was not living as Paul in the Bible tells us: *"be content in whichever situation we are in"* (Philippians 4:11).

Sarah Young, in her devotional, *Jesus Calling*, aptly shares what the Lord spoke to her, "Stop judging and evaluating yourself, for this is not your role. Above all, stop comparing yourself with other people. This produces feelings of pride or inferiority; sometimes, a mixture of both. I lead each of My children along a path that is uniquely tailor-made for him or her. Comparing is not only wrong; it is also meaningless. Don't look for affirmation in the wrong places; your own evaluations, or those of other people. The only source of real affirmation is My unconditional Love." In other words, STOP COMPARING!

Temptation Lies (bait/hook)

The purpose of temptation lies is to entice us to take the "bait." They look innocent and good on the outside so they lure us to open the door and give Satan a foothold. Maybe it sounds or looks like this:

"I'll just try it this one time,"

"I know I'm married, but we're just having a conversation."

"It's just a fantasy story."

"It's not hurting anyone."

Barb had been under a lot of stress with her job. She felt like a failure for a long time because her father always told her she'd never amount to much, and this was her chance to prove herself. An attractive man at work started paying more attention to her. Since her marriage was troubled, she was vulnerable, but figured it wouldn't hurt to have a conversation with him. As time went on their conversations started to get more personal and she found herself thinking of him more and more. She kept telling herself there was really nothing wrong with it because she had not done nothing physically intimate, but she had become emotionally attached. It put a wedge between her and her husband and she started having thoughts of leaving him to pursue a relationship with her work colleague.

I don't know how many times I have fallen for temptation lies, not recognizing them as lies designed to lure me into a trap.

Lies of Conscience – justifying/managing sin

If we give in to the temptation then we begin to justify the lie and the actions or sin we have entered in to. This leads to lies of conscience/justifying/managing sin, which can be similar to the temptation lies, but may sound/look more like this:

"I tried it and it really didn't change me or affect me."

"I'm not addicted to alcohol. I just had a few drinks. I can stop anytime."

"He's such a nice man and he makes me feel special. We don't have a physical relationship. He's just a good friend."

I've seen the justification for emotional and physical infidelity or addiction lock people into a vicious cycle of lies. We often don't want to take responsibility for choices or actions that we know are wrong, so we try to justify ourselves by pretending it really isn't that bad or we couldn't help it. Or, because someone else did something, or often in the case of infidelity, didn't do something we were expecting, we rationalize our sinful choices and actions. Even to the point of playing the victim and feeling sorry for ourselves or blaming others. For example, a woman has an affair with another man, but justifies it by blaming her husband for not paying enough attention to her, or loving her as he should. In her mind, she is the victim in the situation. If her husband had shown more appreciation for her, she wouldn't have had an affair.

Accusatory/Condemning Lies – false identity

These are lies that make us feel condemned, tempt us to believe lies about God or how God views us. They can skew our perception of ourselves, others, and God, leading us to a false or mistaken identity. Here are a few examples:

God doesn't love me

God is just like my earthly father

I'm not worth anything

I would be happy if _____

Sex is love

You may look at some of these and ask, "That's a lie?" That's exactly what Satan would want. If we think it's true then we will more readily take the bait. With some lies, we have heard and believed them for so long, it has become our truth or reality. Other times our culture tells us certain things are true and because everyone else believes it, so do we.

A very pervasive lie is "Sex is love." Sex is meant to be a beautiful expression of love within a marriage, but Satan has used pornography, his counterfeit love, to steal and distort God's initial beautiful design for love and sex.

My introduction to love and sex was through pornography. All my mother had told me was that when sex is with someone you love it's beautiful. My dad was of the "Playboy generation." I was about twelve when I discovered the stack of magazines on the top shelf of his closet. When I was home alone one day my curiosity got the better of me, and as I opened one of the magazines and stepped into a world of beautiful, airbrushed naked women, I was catapulted into deeper depression. I thought to myself, "Is *this* what men expect and desire? Do I have to look like this to ever attract the love of a man?" Looking at those magazines and reading those stories, I thought this was what love was all about. As long as I looked like one of these women, and did these kinds of things with a man, I would be loved and fulfilled in a relationship.

I carried this twisted, deceptive view of love and sex into my adulthood. It caused all kinds of fears and misconceptions in relationships. I had to allow God to wash me clean of all the perverted images and stories I'd seen and read, wrong attitudes and behavior towards men, embrace the truth of His perfect design for love and sex in marriage, and be set free from all the lies and deception.

Another lie I've seen a lot of people struggle with is, "God is just like my earthly Father." For many years I believed this lie. My father was a good and caring man, but he had a habit of promising things and then backing out at the last minute. He almost didn't come to my college graduation because of a business meeting. I would always get my hopes up and think, "This time will be different," and each time it was not. I felt let down over and over again. I believed that my father really didn't love me, and, therefore, God didn't love me either. He would promise me things and at the last minute let me down, just like my father. I couldn't trust my earthy father or God, which spilled over to believing I couldn't trust any man.

Pay attention to what you are hearing and telling yourself and begin to become more aware of the things that tempt you. Ask God to reveal to you lies you have believed.

Before You Read On

1. What kinds of lies are you most apt to believe?

2. Why do you think it is sometimes easier for us to believe a lie than the truth?

3. Pray and ask God to begin to reveal to you the lies you have been believing. * As He reveals them to you, write them down.

4. Now ask the Lord to help you understand how this lie took root in your life.

SUGGESTED PRAYER

Dear Heavenly Father, reveal to me the lies I have believed and as you do help me to understand how they may have taken root in my life and caused me to believe them. Forgive me for believing them and help me to see them as the lies they are and what they have brought into my life. Continue to lead me into Your truth and freedom as I trust you through this journey to my true identity. In Jesus' Name ~ Amen

* *Refer to the "Lies We Believe" list in the resource section at the back of this book.*

Chapter 6
Weighed Down With Lies

I will never be chosen, loved, or cherished.

Remember the example of a day of deception? Well, imagine that when you get out of bed, you put on a large, empty backpack. Each time a lie comes at you, imagine that lie as a heavy book and put it in your backpack. The first lie comes, "I'm fat and ugly and if I'd lose five pounds I would be liked more." Put that one in. The next one, "I'm an undesirable wife and bad mother" goes in, and the next one, "If I looked like that my life would be perfect," the next one, "I have to work hard to prove myself," the next, "I can't do anything right." Is the backpack feeling heavy? Keep adding those lies and drag them around all day long. Your back is starting to hurt and your knees feel weak. It's hard to concentrate, move around your office or drive. Yet you keep the backpack strapped on tight until you climb into bed. Sometimes you even wear it to bed!

I was so weighed down with lies that when I was in my late teens I wrote this in my journal:

"I have felt all my life that people tell me they love me but I have never really felt loved. Many

times I have felt that people would be complimentary just to be nice. Like after my last surgery when someone said they thought I looked very different and later mom said he just said that to be nice. Those things really hurt. I'm really tired of all this pain and I'm tired of keeping up a front. I wish there was someone who would listen to me and would really understand. I don't want to live another day looking the way I do, I don't want to look in the mirror and try to cover up an awful mistake anymore. Oh, I know it could be worse, but I'm the one who has to live with this face all my life. I'm afraid of too many things, too many people, and what they really think. I'm crawling deeper and deeper inside myself. It's easy and sheltered that way. Is this a sign that I could be aiming towards something drastic? I really don't know. I see the world through different eyes because of the defect I was born with. I don't know what it's like to look "normal" and I never will. I will never be chosen, loved, or cherished.

"I need help but I don't know where to turn I don't know where to go. I don't know where to run to. I feel like running away from all my problems. If I were to end it and someone were to find this and read it, I hope that somehow they would understand and I hope God will forgive me. I know this is thought to be a very selfish thing. I know it's not easy for those I leave but somehow you must understand my pain and my wanting to finally be free of societies mocking chains."

As I continued to believe the lie that because I was born with a birth defect I was "damaged" and therefore not worthy of love, and everyone would be better off without me, it drew me into ungodly beliefs and actions that eventually led me down a path to strongholds and bondages. (People pleasing, insecurity, self-pity, addictions, and depression to name a few.) It then became a vicious cycle. The more I believed and acted on the lies, the more I was trapped in strongholds and bondages. The more I was trapped in bondage, the harder it was to see the truth and break free. I was looking for my worth from the world, trying to bind up my wounds and be healed of hurts through worldly solutions. (Approval, performance, food, having nice things, putting others down, etc.) I was wearing that heavy backpack all day long, every day, for YEARS!

The Process Of The Lie *

Satan wants to keep us weighed down with lies and ungodly beliefs that will lead us into strongholds and bondage, eventually destroying us. He is a master at counterfeiting things, making them look good on the outside (the bait) when they contain ruin on the inside (the hook). It's very subtle and not an apparent progression, but a lie can mushroom into a destructive situation. We open the door, step inside and before we know it, we are locked into an area of stronghold or bondage, wondering, "How did I get here?"

Romans 1:25 tells us that *"they exchanged the truth about God for a lie."*

FIRST, we HEAR a lie. A lie will come through the world (media, people, Satan etc.), or our own thoughts, and gradually develop into ungodly beliefs and behavior patterns. Some say, "You are what you eat." I say, "You are what you think/believe." This is why it is so crucial to "take every thought captive to Christ."

SECOND, we RECEIVE the lie. We can choose to receive it or reject it. If we don't recognize it as a lie we are more likely to receive it and give Satan a foothold (Ephesians 4:27, *"and do not give the devil a foothold"* NIV.). We may hear a lie in our mind, such as "Since you are really introverted, no one likes you and you will never have any friends." If we then choose to receive it, we accept it as truth and internalize it.

THIRD, we will begin to BELIEVE it. Believing lies will lead to ungodly thoughts, and if we continue to receive it or internalize it, we will begin to believe it as truth.

FOURTH, we will begin to ACT on the LIE. If we believe a lie, we will eventually act on it. This will lead to ungodly actions which will lead to painful emotions such as fear, anger, anxiety, unforgiveness, hurting others and even physical issues.

FINALLY, we will end up in BONDAGE to the lie and the behavior the lie has caused. Because the lie has now become "our truth," we operate out of a false reality and false self. We don't recognize the lie, we just know we are experiencing pain and trouble, struggling with addictions, feeling trapped, and don't know how to get out.

* See the "Lies Progression Chart" in the Resources section in the back of this book.

Boyd Bailey tells us in *Wisdom Hunters Devotional*, "Strongholds are Satan's attempt to strangle spiritual life out of the saints of God. The enemy is not slack in his attacks; indeed he is always on the prowl to pronounce judgment and dispense shame. Some of his strategic strongholds are pride, addiction, and self-absorption. He sucks in a susceptible heart and a wandering mind with alluring sin. The devil builds a faithless fortress and launches missiles of doubt with false ideologies.

"How do strongholds take hold and grow in our life? Ironically, a strength can become a stronghold. Healthy confidence drifts into arrogance. The gift of discernment grows into a judgmental attitude. The discipline to work out regularly and eat right becomes an obsession that consumes every minute of our discretionary time. The goal to get ahead financially grows into greed and a sense of superiority. A strength can be a stronghold, so always be alert.

"The Lord is good—Satan is bad. The Lord clarifies—Satan confuses. The Lord offers freedom—Satan enlists bondage. The Lord gives grace—Satan pours on guilt. The Lord forgives—Satan shames. The Lord creates contentment—Satan drives for more. The Lord loves people—Satan hates people. The Lord wants what's best for you—Satan wants what's worst for you. The Lord gives—Satan takes."

2 Peter 2:19 tells us, *"For whatever overcomes a person, to that he is enslaved."*

Satan works this way to draw people into a substance addiction. It almost never starts as an addiction. It starts with one drink, one bite, one drag, one pill, one look. And one step at a time you are drawn into full blown dependence.

Satan wants us so weighed down with lies that we are convinced no one understands us, no one loves us, there is no way out, and we have no hope. But remember Satan's true motives. He wants us dragging through life staring at our toes in worry and depression, leading us to live in a "mistaken identity," looking to the world for solutions instead of to God.

Before You Read On

1. What lies are in your "backpack?"

2. How distorted is your thinking? How many "could-have," "would-have," "should-have" statements have you made today? How many "if only" were part of your inner vocabulary today? Do you ever make comments like "nothing ever goes right for me;" "everything I touch fails;" "I always mess up?"

3. Are you putting the "backpack" on each morning and carrying it around all day long? What impact is that having on you mentally, emotionally, physically, and spiritually?

4. Define stronghold and bondage in your own words.

5. Lies are at the root of every area of bondage or stronghold. From the lies that God has revealed to you, can you see how they may have led to an area of bondage or stronghold?

6. Write down a lie that you have believed and how that lie manifested itself in each step of the "process of the lie," and what stronghold or bondage it may have led you to.

SUGGESTED PRAYER

Dear Heavenly Father, please forgive me for the areas of bondage I have been enslaved to and the lies that have led to sinful behavior patterns. Help me to surrender totally to you and trust you to lead me out of the destructive habits, to stand firm in You, flee temptation and run toward holiness. And as I take these steps bring strength, healing and wholeness in YOU. In Jesus' Name ~ Amen

Art Director days. 1982-1985

Chapter 7
Mistaken Identity

I wonder who the REAL me is?

I couldn't wait to tell my dad that I had been offered the position of Art Director for the Billy Graham Evangelistic Association. At last I had accomplished something that would make him proud of me. My goal in life was to become an art director like my father, and I had done it by age twenty-five! If I couldn't be beautiful, I could be talented and successful in the things he liked and knew. Maybe then he would love me more.

I believed this lie for most of my late teen and early adult years. I built an entire life and identity around the lie that my worth was based on my performance, since it couldn't be found in my physical appearance. Believing this lie led to strongholds and bondages.

The Ugly Duckling story is a classic case of a mistaken identity. I, too, had a mistaken identity. I had been looking to what I had accomplished, or what others thought of me and said about me, to find my identity. I let those things define me. I was looking to people and the world for affirmation and acceptance, and I, like the ugly duckling, didn't know who I *really* was.

My teenage daughter believed the lie that no one likes an introvert. She felt "invisible," overlooked, and unpopular. She felt she had to become something she was not—outgoing and bubbly—in order to be noticed, accepted, and loved. However, this idealized personality was so different from her natural one that she knew donning it would be impossible. Instead, she believed that if she became the best student in her class, she could get others to notice and admire her. She began to work harder in school, take on extra assignments, and volunteer to lead groups and organizations. She felt she had to be smarter than everyone else and would get depressed if she earned less than an A. She was determined to prove her worth to others. She built her whole identity on lies. She, too, was locked into a mistaken identity.

Identity

Let's back up a minute and define "identity" and "mistaken." *Dictionary.com* defines identity as: 1. The fact of being who or what a person or thing is. 2. The state or fact of remaining the same one or ones, as under varying aspects or conditions. 3. The condition of being oneself or itself and not another. 4. The distinct personality of an individual regarded as a persisting entity; individuality.

And *Thesaurus.com's* other words for identity are: character, distinctiveness, existence, identification, integrity, name, oneness, particularity, personality, self, selfhood, singularity, uniqueness.

Mistaken is defined by *Dictionary.com* as: 1. wrongly conceived, held, or done 2. erroneous; incorrect; wrong 3. having made a mistake; being in error.

These definitions show us that our identity is unique to us and delineates who and what we are. God tells us in Psalm 139:13-14 that He *"formed my inward parts; knitted me together in my mother's womb, that I am fearfully and wonderfully made."* There is no one in the world exactly like us. However, Satan wants us to believe that we need to be like everyone else to be loved and accepted, live up to certain cultural standards and expectation that our "mistaken identity" is our true identity.

"And What Do You Do?"

When we meet someone new, after we exchange names, what do we say? "And what do you DO?" Try describing yourself without mentioning what you DO. Tough, isn't it? We often answer by saying what type of job we have, where we live, what school we go to, how many kids we have, what kind of car we drive, what activities we enjoy, or what church we go to. We are telling others what we are instead of who we are. Did you notice the definition of identity and similar words to describe identity? All talk about uniqueness and personhood. It does not mention what one does as a definition of identity.

What is your source of identity? Is it in what you do? Your job, role as a husband/wife, father/mother, son/daughter, student, your talents or abilities, your accomplishments? Or perhaps it's in what you have? Your house, your car, your clothes, your toys, your education and degrees? Is it your looks, or what others say about you? Often we get our identity from many of these sources.

I can look back over my life and see all the different sources I looked to for my identity. It changed whenever I entered a different season of life, and then as I grew older many of the sources overlapped. It started with being a daughter. Since I felt I had to earn the love of my parents, especially my father, I was obedient and compliant. I then became a student. I tried to be a perfect student, thinking it would bring me acceptance and approval. I also strived to be the best at whatever sport I played. Then I began working. I tried to be the most dedicated, creative, and successful employee, along with trying to keep up with the latest fashions. Then I got married. Now I was going to be the greatest wife ever! I was going to be the model of love, patience, support, and respect to my husband. Then I became a mother and poured all I could into being an exemplary parent. I was going to have perfect children and everyone would think highly of me. Then I became a ministry leader. Now I was "working for God" so I would do my best to do it all perfectly and gain the admiration of others and God. It was easy to let my identity become what I did for God instead of who I was in God.

We are all looking for identity, a sense of significance, love and acceptance. We are born with this longing in our hearts that only God can fill. (Ecclesiastes 3:11 … *He also has planted eternity in men's hearts and minds [a divinely implanted sense of a purpose working through the ages which nothing under the sun but God alone can satisfy* (AMP).

Broken Mirrors

"Some of us have lived in an emotional prison because we have accepted what a false 'broken' mirror said to us about ourselves." - Nancy Leigh DeMoss

Sarah experienced this. She let kids' treatment of her in high school define who she was into her early fifties. She felt because she was not popular and well liked, that there was something wrong with her. She believed that about herself, let it define her, and carried that into her adult life!

Galatians 1:10 tells us, *"For am I now seeking the approval of men, or of God?"*

Is your main source of identity from what others say about you or what you assume they think of you? I was constantly seeking the approval and affirmation of "man." I was always concerned about what others thought or said about me. If they said I was "ugly or stupid or worthless," I believed them. Even after I became a Christian I was still more concerned about what others thought of me than what God did. I was a total people pleaser. I, too, was looking into a "broken mirror," locked into the reflection of a mistaken identity. *"Man looks at the outward appearance, but the LORD looks on the heart"* (1 Samuel 16:7).

In looking for approval from man instead of God, I was afraid of letting others see the real me. Every morning I would get up, put my suit and mask on and hide behind my job. I could receive accolades for a job well done, and no one had to know what was going on inside of me or what I had been through. I could handle rejection related to my work, but not to me personally. Because I wanted man's approval, I became a workaholic. I was a rat running around inside a wheel, spinning but never getting anywhere, trapped in a cycle of a mistaken identity.

This cycle led to being fearful, withdrawn, and depressed. I held back affection for fear of being rejected, and I didn't trust anyone. I had walls a mile high around myself. But those walls of protection also kept out the thing I longed for the most: unconditional love and acceptance.

Our life situation is important and says something about us, our abilities, accomplishments, and passions. But when it becomes the source of our identity, it is based on a fragile, man-centered, man-fearing source. When we let the world define who we are, it's like going out into a raging storm with no protection and expecting not to get wet.

Before You Read On

1. Tell someone about yourself without telling them what you *do*.

2. How does our culture define and influence how we see ourselves?

3. What things do we draw our identity from?

4. Where are you getting your identity? Have you been looking for your identity from the wrong source(s)? Can you identify what some of those wrong sources have been?

5. How does believing lies, wanting to please others, be accepted by others, or have other's approval cause us to seek our identity from the wrong sources and lead us into a mistaken identity?

6. Are you caught in the cycle of a mistaken identity?

SUGGESTED PRAYER

Dear Heavenly Father, thank you that before I was formed in the womb, You had me in mind and created me just as I am. Help me to delight in and accept my uniqueness and to realize the wonderful truth that I am unlike anyone else you ever made! Help me to understand the ways I have been living with a mistaken identity and begin to see my reflection from YOUR mirror, the correct source of my true identity. In Jesus' name.
~ Amen

Around age 37

Chapter 8
Breaking the Chains

*I want so badly to be freed of
this bondage of depression.*

As I stood up to share my story, I was shaking like a leaf. My knees were knocking, my palms were sweaty, and I wasn't sure I could speak without freezing up. I really, really, *really* didn't want to tell it. My voice was a bit squeaky but a few sentences in, God filled me with His calm. I cautiously shared my story and then waited for the tidal wave of rejection to come. But as I looked out over the group of women they were speechless, passing the Kleenex around and applauding. I was stunned. *The chains of believing a lie for over twenty-nine years were broken!* I felt a huge part of my soul healed. An enormous weight lifted off of me. I felt FREE. Then I started crying.

Road To Freedom

The path to sharing my story was long and arduous. When I was thirty-five I was still convinced that I would always be thought of as ugly, unlovable, broken, depressed, and worthless. I kept telling myself to be strong and not so afraid of rejection. Fear had gripped me all my life and I was battle-weary. And this was after I had received Christ. I was not instantly free of my troubles or the bondages I had been in for years.

The road to freedom is a journey. But I deeply discouraged by the fact that even after being a Christian for so many years I was still battling doubts, fear, and depression. I felt like a spiritual failure. What was I doing wrong? Why couldn't I feel free and joyful? I knew God could set me free, but it wasn't happening. I was still carrying that heavy backpack filled with crippling lies. How could I get it off my back and *keep* it off? How could I exchange lies and mistaken identity for complete freedom in my true identity in Christ?

My husband and older daughter were volunteers with the forest service in Southern California for a few years and part of their work was to patrol the hiking trails. I would watch them load up their backpacks with all kinds of nifty equipment and comment, "That looks heavy, how do you get it on and off?" My husband told me it was best from a kneeling position, not standing. That made sense.

I acknowledged the first step in getting the backpack full of lies off is to kneel in surrender before the Lord. Had I truly surrendered in all areas of my life? Was I being prideful, fearful, and doubtful? Is that why I was still carrying this heavy load of lies around? As I looked back I began to see areas where I had not, and still was not, completely surrendered to God.

"No Way, Lord!"

When I was twenty, sitting by a river near my college, God told me that someday He was going to use my story. I thought, "Well that's nice, but I'm just never going to be ready." I still didn't talk much, and the thought of standing in front of a group of people and exposing my life to them was terrifying. The lie Satan told me was, *"If you tell your story you will experience the ultimate rejection like you never have before."* I was locked in that lie for twenty-nine years. Believing that lie, I resisted God's desire for me to share my story.

God, being the wonderful, loving Father that He is, led me with baby steps. I was frequently asked to be on a panel or to speak on general topics. Things I felt comfortable talking about and did not reveal the real me. I didn't have to take my mask all the way off. However, each time I spoke someone came up to me after my talk and told me they thought I had a gift for public speaking. I thanked them and blew it off. *"Not going to work, God. Not telling it."*

This went on for quite a few years. Then one day a friend handed me a brochure about a Christian speaker's seminar and said she really thought I should go. I told her I would pray about it and if God provided the funds for me to go, I would. A few weeks later, a friend who heard me mention it sent me a check with a note saying, "I'm glad God is calling you to tell your story and not mine!" Well, now I had to go.

The seminar was three, life-changing days. Not only did I gain invaluable tools for speaking, I was assured that God could make any personality type a good speaker, even introverts like me, and was convinced that I should tell my story. I made an agreement with God that if He opened the door for me to speak, I would walk through it.

God opened many doors for me to speak, and as I had promised, I walked through them, but I knew that I was holding out on Him, still fearful and not trusting Him completely. I continued to believe the lie about ultimate rejection, and only shared certain parts of my story.

Then about thirteen years after I attended the speaker's seminar I was asked to serve as the women's ministry director at my church in Southern California. As I started to pray about what we should do for an upcoming women's retreat, God very clearly spoke into my spirit, *"I want you to share your story. You are ready."* I panicked and thought, *"No way, Lord."* He told me I had run out of excuses.

I knew I had to stop running. At last I surrendered and asked Him to help me creatively tell my story and break through my paralyzing fear. He gave me the True Identity message, an innovative way to share it, and assurance that I would not experience rejection but acceptance.

That was exactly what happened when I fully shared my story for the first time at the retreat. God gave me what I needed to break through the lie and fear that had gripped me for so many years!

Another amazing thing happened after I shared my story that day. Women started sharing their stories with one another. Women who had known each other for over ten years shared things they had never shared before! Telling my story had broken the power of the lie of rejection in other women's lives.

At the end of the retreat the women told me, "Jennifer, when we saw you sitting up in the front row as the pastor's wife and women's ministry director, we thought you were well educated and had it all together. We weren't sure how to relate to you. After sharing your story with us today we realize that you're just like us. You've hurt just like us and experienced difficult things just like we have. You gave us permission to take off our masks and be real with one another. Thank you!"

Healing often comes after sharing. A lot of healing happened that day!

Fear will try to keep you from fully surrendering, but the Lord tells us *"perfect love casts out all fear"* (1 John 4:18). Every time I'm facing fear, I tell myself this verse, this TRUTH, and allow God to help me press through the fear, peel off one more layer of lies, and bring deeper healing.

Get To The Root

All areas of stronghold and bondage originate in some sort of lie. In order to break free of these prisons, we first need to recognize the lie at their core. Jeremiah 17:9-10 tells us *"the heart is deceitful"* and asks the Lord to *"search the heart and test the mind."* 2 Corinthians 3:16-17 states, *"But when one turns to the Lord, the veil is removed. Now the Lord is the Spirit, and where the spirit of the Lord is, there is freedom."*

In order to recognize a lie, we must first know God's truth. How do we identify counterfeit things? Do bankers study hundreds of examples of counterfeit money to recognize it? No, they study the real thing. They study it so well that when something that is not real comes across their desk they will say, "Wait a minute! Something is not right with this one." It is the same with distinguishing lies.

Ask God to search you, to "remove the veil" and reveal to you the lies you have believed. Begin to evaluate what is going on around you and in you. Ask when you hear something, "What is the real message here? Is it really true? Am I being deceived in a way contrary to God's truth?"

Joan had spent years working her way up the corporate ladder, chasing after the "American Dream." She had a devoted husband, two kids, a dog, great salary, a large home, a luxury car, and was well liked. She had made it to the top! But there was a price to pay for this "dream." She had to keep working to maintain the dream and always have the best. She traveled constantly, putting a strain on her marriage and family life. They longed to have time with her, but when she was home she was not really present. Her mind was always on work-related issues.

The dream was shattered one Friday evening when she returned from a trip and her husband told her he couldn't go on like this anymore. She had to choose between her career and her family.

Joan's identity was all about her job and the "stuff" that went with it. She loved the recognition and perks, the big house, nice clothes, and luxury car. But as she chased after "the dream," she was losing the thing she loved the most: her family. She began to recognize the lie and trap of this dream.

God dramatically turned Joan's life around. She came to a saving relationship with Christ, left her job, and began to restore her family relationships. As she got to know the truth of who she really was in God's Word, the world lost its attractive allure. She is now helping others draw closer to God and find their fulfillment and identity in a relationship with Christ, not their job or bank account.

Another helpful tool in identifying a lie is realizing what sets off your emotions. What makes you feel fearful, angry, hurt, depressed?

Cindy came to me in tears, upset that someone had said something to Cindy and then ignored her during a table discussion time. As she talked, I realized that the other woman had triggered a wounded spot in Cindy. The woman had not ignored Cindy, but because she had used a particular word that held a place of woundedness in Cindy, it had hurt her.

I encouraged Cindy that the woman did not try to hurt her, but that Cindy is sensitive because of something that happened to her earlier in her life. She was able to trace the hurt back to the lie that her opinion did not matter, written on her heart years ago by her father.

She later told me that was a turning point for her to begin to take a closer look at what sets off her emotions and trace it back to an original lie, instead of wallowing in the lie. She was able to let go of the hurt, enjoy the rest of the weekend with her table group, and feel included in the discussions.

The Lie Barometer

"There is therefore now no condemnation for those who are in Christ Jesus" (Romans 8:1).

I call this verse, Romans 8:1, the "Lie Barometer."

Let's take a look at the difference between condemnation and conviction.

Condemnation is strong censure, reproof, and disapproval, bringing on shame, guilt, and accusation. Conviction means convicted or being convicted, firm belief.

Conviction says, "I did something wrong."

Condemnation says, "There is something wrong with me."

Conviction brings appropriate guilt from sin and condemnation produces shame.

This verse says there is NO condemnation for those who are in Christ Jesus. In our sin we do deserve to be punished, but Christ paid the penalty for our sins on the cross. HE took on all our condemnation. Therefore, if you are trusting Christ, yet feeling condemned, you know it is not from God. Satan, the Father of Lies, condemns, and wants you to believe that the lie and the sin it leads to is your identity.

The Holy Spirit convicts. He will firmly and gently point out the areas in our lives that need correction and change. It is always for our good, to make us more like Christ, for the good of others who may be involved, and ultimately to glorify Himself!

When you understand the difference between the two, the next time you hear something that makes you feel condemned, recognize it as a lie. Even if it is someone else saying it to you. Satan often uses others to bring lies into our lives.

When my mother became ill with leukemia, she was convinced that God was punishing her because she was "such a bad person." She had lived under condemnation from her mother for many years, told that when bad things happen to people it is because they are bad or have done something bad. She was sure that her mother's criticism was true and she deserved to be punished.

I read scripture to her to reinforce the truth that because of what Christ did for her on the cross, she was forgiven, free, and righteous in His sight. A treasured daughter of the King. She eventually embraced the truth of who and whose she was and found peace in the midst of a very frightening, uncertain time.

I've heard many stories from women who have suffered horrible abuse. They tell me they lived under the condemnation of the abuser and believed if they ever told anyone they would pay dearly. They were told that the abuse was their fault, they were worthless trash, they deserved it and no one would ever love them. After a while they believed it and saw themselves this way, convinced this is who they were. As they began to recognize these condemning words as lies, they began to move toward truth and freedom as beloved daughters of God.

Renounce The Lie

"For the grace of God has appeared, bringing salvation for all people, training us to renounce ungodliness and worldly passions, and to live self-controlled, upright, and godly lives in the present age" (Titus 2: 11-12).

Once you recognize the lie, you need to *renounce* it. Speaking out the lie helps break its hold on you. For instance, I have at times while driving, or in other places by myself, as a lie comes into my thoughts, said out loud, "That's a LIE!" "I renounce the lie that I am rejected, unloved or shameful. In Christ *I am accepted.*" "I renounce the lie that I am worthless, inadequate, inferior, or hopeless. In Christ *I am significant.*" When I speak the lie out loud and renounce it, I am able to let it go and embrace God's truth.

My dad was eighty-six years old and near the end of his life. He was searching desperately for truth and understanding of life, heaven, and God. He read books, listened to tapes, read the Bible, but was having a hard time getting past feeling God was distant and didn't care about him personally. He said to me one evening after he had been diagnosed with terminal lung cancer, "I wish I could talk to God and hear from God like you and your brothers do." I told him he could. He said, "No, God only talks to priests and 'religious' people like you guys." I told him that was a LIE, that Satan did not want him to believe that he could have a close walk with God, but that God was longing for a personal relationship with him. All those years of the lies that God was distant and uncaring were finally renounced and broken. I led him through a salvation prayer that evening. He passed away just two weeks later. I know he's had many very *special, intimate* conversations with God and will for eternity!

Go The Other Direction

Neil Anderson, who has written many excellent books about freedom in Christ says, "Even though Satan is defeated, he still rules this world through a hierarchy of demons who tempt, accuse, and deceive those who fail to put on the armor of God, stand firm in their faith, and take every thought captive to the obedience of Christ. Our sanctuary is our identity and position in Christ, and we have all the protection we need to live victorious lives; BUT if we fail to assume our responsibility and give ground to the Satan, we will suffer the consequences of our sinful attitudes, and actions. The Good news is, we can repent and reclaim all that we have in Christ."

Once we RECOGNIZE the lie and RENOUNCE the lie, we must REPENT of the lie and sinful attitudes and actions it led to. Repent doesn't just mean to say, "I'm sorry." Repentance means to turn around and go the other direction. We must make a change for the better as a result of remorse or contrition for our sins. *"Repent therefore, and turn again, that your sins may be blotted out, that times of refreshing may come from the presence of the Lord"* (Acts 3:19).

Before You Read On

1. Are you having a difficult time leaving the backpack at the foot of the cross? What is keeping you from kneeling in surrender to remove the backpack?

2. Do you understand the difference between conviction and condemnation? Are you feeling condemned in some area of your life? Can you begin to recognize the lie that is bringing the condemnation?

3. What sets off your emotions? (Fear, anxiety, hurt, guilt, shame, anger, depression, etc.) What are your "trigger" points? Ask God to reveal to you the root lies that are at the core of these emotions.

4. Ask God to forgive you of the thought patterns and sinful behavior the lies may have led to, and to give you the strength to stop believing and giving in to the lies.

5. As God may continue to reveal lies to you, repeat the steps of Recognizing the Lie, Renouncing the Lie, and Repenting of the sinful actions the Lie may have led to. Be refreshed and move on in Christ!

SUGGESTED PRAYER

Dear Heavenly Father, please help me to fully surrender all areas of my life to You. Help me to begin to recognize the lies I have believed and to then renounce them and repent of the behavior believing them may have led to. Help me to also recognize the difference between Your conviction and Satan' condemnation in my life. Lord, search me and show me my trigger points and what sets off my emotions so I may begin to be aware of the core lies that trigger my ungodly emotions and beliefs. Continue the process of setting me free from strongholds and bondages. Move my "knowing" to "believing" Your Truth . In Jesus' Name ~ Amen

My handsome brothers and I with our grandfather.

Chapter 9
Throwing Off the Backpack

*If Satan comes knocking on your door,
ask Jesus to answer it!*

Picture yourself with that heavy backpack on, kneeling down, surrendered at the foot of the cross, unbuckling the strap around your waist, and taking it off. Unzip the top and begin to unpack each book and lay it at the foot of the cross. As you remove each book, counter the lie on the book with God's truth.

When I read Neil Anderson's book *Victory Over the Darkness* I first grasped this concept. He explains that we need to have a *Truth Encounter*. We need to counter and replace every lie with God's TRUTH. You see, I had been trying to "talk myself" out of feeling bad. I would say, "That's a lie," but I left it at that. But after reading the book, I finally understood what the verse *"take every thought captive to obey Christ"* (2 Corinthians 10:5) and *"you will know the TRUTH and the TRUTH will set you free,"* (John 8:32) meant. When a lie came into my thoughts or sight, I needed to take that lie to Christ—"When Satan comes knocking, ask Jesus to answer it"—

"take every thought captive," and counter each lie with God's truth – His Word. It was GOD's TRUTH that would set me free, not me trying to reason my way through it, give myself another pep talk, or tell myself I shouldn't feel this way. God has given us truth in His Word to counter EVERY lie, but we need to apply it, not just read it or memorize it. God has given us His truth since the beginning of time, knowing our adversary, Satan, better than any other, and what we need to win the battles with him.

Here's some of what was in my backpack and a truth to counter each lie.

I CAN'T TRUST ANYONE – Matthew 6:25, 33 - God is faithful; He will take care of me. *"Seek first the kingdom of God and His righteousness, and all these things will be added to you."*

GOD DOESN'T LOVE ME – 1 John 3:1 - God loves me greatly.

I'M NOT WORTH ANYTHING – Deuteronomy 14:2 - I am God's treasured possession.

PHYSICAL BEAUTY MATTERS MORE THAN INWARD BEAUTY – 1 Samuel 16:7 - *"Man looks at the outward appearance but the LORD looks on the heart."*

I WOULD BE HAPPY IF _____. Philippians 4:11- My joy comes from knowing God.

I'M INFERIOR, A NOBODY – John 1:12 - I am a child of the King.

I CAN'T DO ANYTHING RIGHT – Philippians 4:13 - *"I can do all things through Christ who strengthens me"* (NKJ).

IT'S HOPELESS – Luke 1:37 – Nothing is impossible for God.*

Leave those books (lies) at the foot of the cross. Let Jesus deal with them. Remember it is not a power encounter with Satan that will set us free from bondage, but a *truth* encounter, through the power of the Holy Spirit within us.

Neil Anderson says, "God has changed our nature, but our responsibility is to change our behavior." As we learn more about the TRUTH of whom GOD says we are (His beloved children) and know how HE views us, our TRUE IDENTITY, we are able to change our thinking and behavior.

We are not to believe evil spirits, nor are we to dialogue with them. Instead, we are to ignore them and choose the truth. You're equipped with the armor of God; they can't touch you unless you drop your guard. For every arrow of temptation, accusation or deception they shoot at you, simply raise the shield of faith, deflect the attack, and walk on. Take every thought captive to the obedience of Christ.

I wrote the words "God's Truth" on an eraser and have it on my desk as a reminder that God's Truth erases every lie that has been written on my heart.

* Refer to "Lies We Believe with Scriptural Truth to Counter" in the Resources section in the back of this book.

Reprogram The Computer

If you change your mind (thinking)
it will change your heart.

Our thinking impacts our physical and spiritual well-being, our souls. As you learn more of God's Word you will see how often He talks about renewing our minds, and how important it is to think on these things—whatever is true, honorable, just, pure, lovely, commendable, excellent, things worthy of praise. (Philippians 4:8) As we saturate our minds with God's truth, it will change our hearts, attitudes, and behavior. He will transform us. He will set us free!

> Romans 12:2 – *"Do not be conformed to this world, but be transformed by the renewal of your mind, that by testing you may discern what is the will of God, what is good and acceptable and perfect."*
>
> Ephesians 4:23 – *"To be made new in the attitude of your minds"* (NIV).
>
> Colossians 3:2 – *"Set your mind on things above, not on earthly things"* (NIV).

Fear Versus Faith

Another major step in being set free in our True Identity is to replace fear-based thinking with faith-based thinking. Not only does fear-based thinking eventually impact you physically, emotionally, and spiritually, it will also keep you in strongholds and bondages. Psalm 56:3

reminds us, *"When I am afraid, I put my trust in You."* Psalm 112:7 says, *"He is not afraid of news; his heart is firm, trusting in the LORD,"* and 2 Timothy 1:7 *"For God has not given us a spirit of fear; but of power, and of love, and of a sound mind"* (KJV).

I recently experienced learning to replace fear-based thinking with faith-based thinking in a very tangible way. I had lived with a gripping fear of getting cancer ever since I watched my mother die a slow and painful death from leukemia when I was twenty-five. She was just fifty-two. I was now fifty-four. I had already had an ovarian cancer scare six years prior, in which I didn't handle the possibility of having cancer well. I had surgery and everything was fine, but the whole experience really rattled me. I was convinced that getting cancer was not an "if" but a "when and what type?" Sooner or later my number would come up.

The day before I was to leave for Kenya on a mission trip, I had a follow-up mammogram and ultrasound on a breast lump I had felt. I was told by the radiologist, "It's not a cyst. I'm not going to lie to you, I am very concerned." I looked at her and felt unphased and completely calm. She asked if I could postpone my trip and have a biopsy the next day. I said, "No, I have to be on that plane to Kenya. I'll be back in three weeks. Can we do it then?" She hesitantly agreed as long as I promised to set up the biopsy appointment before I left the office.

As I sat in the nurse's office waiting for her to set up the biopsy appointment, I said, "Lord, this must be that peace 'that passes all understanding' (Philippians 4:7) because I do not feel afraid! THANK YOU for filling me with your peace! Please keep me in this place. Help me to have faith and trust you in this." I knew about this peace but had never experienced it in this way.

The nurse reassured me that waiting three weeks for the biopsy was not a problem. She encouraged me to go on the trip and not let this occupy my thoughts or concerns. I told her I knew God was with me and I was going to be okay no matter what happened. She hugged me and told me she would be praying for me.

I went to Kenya and appreciated each moment and experience. One morning I sat overlooking the Serengeti Plain from our safari camp, and thought, "Thank you, Lord, for allowing me to experience this. If I never get to come back to Kenya or see any of these people or places again, thank you for this gift. Thank you for the gift of life and gift of YOU. Thank you for your continued peace. Thank you that I am not afraid." I did not tell anyone on my mission team about the cancer possibility. I didn't want that to take away from what God had for this trip and for all of us. I didn't even tell my older daughter who was traveling with me. God kept me in His perfect peace the entire trip (including one week in Holland on the way home to visit my husband's family) and I had the most amazing, life-changing experiences.

Two days after I returned I had the breast biopsy. Three days after that I received a call from the radiologist asking, "Do you have a moment to talk?" (It's never a good sign when the radiologist calls and wants to "talk.") I braced myself. She said it was good news and bad. The bad news was that it was cancer; the good news was we caught it early and she felt I was going to be fine. She then very matter-of-factly gave me instructions for next steps and the phone number of a breast surgeon. I hung up the phone and just sat there in silence. Shocked, but not fearful or worried, and surprised I was not freaking out. I called my husband and told him the news. He asked if I needed him to come home and I said, "No, I'm okay. We can talk more later." We told our girls later that day. They said, "Mom, you don't seem worried, so we're not worried." I made some jokes about what I would do if I lost my hair and we assured one another we would all trust the Lord to get us through this. I was choosing faith and I was remarkably still at peace.

I was launched into the "Pink Ribbon Club" overnight and embarked on an intensely challenging rollercoaster ride for the next five months of tests and treatment. There were many very dark and bleak times in which I didn't want to face another day, but God was in the center of the storm and He assured me I was going to be okay. He surrounded me with incredible love, prayer, support, and help, and gave me all I needed to keep going. Especially all those days I dragged myself to radiation treatment, and days I went to the gym for a session with my trainer. My doctors had said that exercise was one of the best things I could do to increase my energy and stamina through radiation treatment, but they specified how much exercise. I figured just getting to the gym and back was a huge accomplishment!

God reminded me that I had been praying to be freed of the fear of cancer, and that the only way for me to experience and know that freedom was to go through it in God's truth and assurance, see Him give me His deep peace in the midst of it, see faith win over fear. I realized that I was not my mother and would not necessarily experience what she did, that no matter what happened to me God was going to carry me through. Even if death was the end result, I would be with Him in heaven. He had prepared me for this journey through many years of being a patient, and I sensed He was going to use me as His ambassador in the medical community. He did. He gave me numerous opportunities to share my faith and people often commented on how at peace I seemed to be. One woman said, "I thought either you were a really good actress or God really has given you His deep peace." I assured her it was the latter.

Looking back just a few months on the other side of this, I was growing even deeper in my understanding of what Paul meant when he said in 1 John 4:18 that *"perfect love casts out fear."* As well as what it looks like to "take every thought captive to Christ" as I mentioned earlier. Experiencing God's perfect love, truth, promises, assurances, and peace set me free from the fear of cancer, just like it had set me free from the fear of rejection a few years prior.

Keep looking to Jesus! Stay in His Word and continue to saturate your mind (reprogram your computer) with His truth. It is said that it takes thirty days to establish a pattern or new habit. It can take longer to undo a bad habit or pattern, but spend thirty days telling yourself the truth and you can begin to believe it and set new patterns.

Stockholm Syndrome

Cathy was having trouble leaving her backpack at the foot of the cross. I heard someone explain this in a very poignant way at one of our retreats. She told us about the "Stockholm Syndrome," a psychological phenomenon wherein hostages express adulation and have positive feelings for their captors. These feelings are usually considered irrational in light of the danger or risk endured by the victims, who essentially mistake a lack of abuse from their captors as an act of kindness. The Stockholm Syndrome is named after the Norrmalmstorg robbery of a bank in Stockholm, in which the bank robbers held bank employees hostage from August 23 to August 28, 1973. The victims became emotionally attached to their captors and even defended them after they were freed from their six-day ordeal. The term "Stockholm Syndrome" was coined by the criminologist and psychiatrist Nils Bejerot, who assisted the police during the robbery.

We keep putting the backpack on and going for another hike with Satan (the captor). One woman told me she did this for years. She got comfortable with her alcohol addiction. She knew how to "do drunk," but was terrified of trying to live sober. Even though she was putting her young children at risk and was enslaved to this terrible bondage, she did not want to take the backpack off and leave it at the foot of the cross. It was not until she got help detoxing and learned new ways to cope with her fears and addiction through Christ, countering the lies she was entrapped in with God's truth, that she was finally set free.

Keep your eyes fixed on Christ. Don't look back, like Lot's wife did as they fled Sodom. Do we look forward and trust Jesus, or keep looking back, longing to be back with the captor? Pray 2 Timothy 2:26—*"and that they will come to their senses and escape from the trap of the devil, who has taken them captive to do his will"* (NIV).

Identity Crisis

When you lay that backpack at the foot of the cross and walk away, you may experience a bit of an identity crisis. You were so used to living in lies they had become your truth. You grew comfortable with them. You were deceived into thinking it was good and right and true, as the women did with their captors. You got emotionally attached to the captor and that way of living. It can be scary to let go of old habits, sinful patterns, and wrong thinking. A counselor once told me, "Jennifer, your 'computer' (mind) has been programmed with lies for so many years, you need to 'reprogram' it with God's truth." That takes time. In between living in the lie and embracing the truth, stepping out of the darkness into the light is a process. It can be very unsettling, and you may not know who you are for awhile.

Keep moving toward the TRUTH of who and whose God says you are! 1 Timothy 3:9 – *"They must keep hold of the deep truths of the faith with a clear conscience"* (NIV).

My husband had been in ministry for twenty-one years when he left a pastorate in Southern California to move to Georgia, in faith, not knowing what was next for him. He went excited for the new ministry opportunities he was sure the Lord had for him there. He soon became the "network king" and met all kinds of people in ministries and churches as he searched for his next assignment. He found nothing. For eighteen months, nothing. God closed every door. My husband went through a major identity crisis, because his identity had always been as pastor, ministry director, or chaplain, and now he didn't know who he was.

As God showed him that He wanted a father-son relationship with him, not a business relationship as it had been, he began to understand and embrace his TRUE identity as God's son. He saw that no matter what he was "doing" he was primarily God's son, and that was where he had to find his solid source of identity.

After eighteen months God did open a door, working as an IT help desk analyst for the Coca Cola International support desk because he spoke Dutch! At first he was crushed. This was the furthest thing from ministry he could think of. Or so he believed. God gave him opportunity to get out from behind a pulpit and be in the marketplace, experiencing a work week like all those people sitting in the church pews he preached to each Sunday. He understood their world and learned to bring God to them.

Eventually God opened another door as Citizen's Advocate and Safety Chaplain for the city we were living in. God has brought him to a place where he now pastors a city, with all new insight, understanding, compassion, and heart, as His son!

Sharon was also going through an identity crisis. She was raised with men, to be a man. She learned to hunt, shoot, talk the talk, and she always worked with men. She was comfortable around men but terrified to be around women. She felt insecure, intimidated, not feminine enough, and thought women didn't like her. She didn't know how to talk about or do "girly" things and had no girlfriends.

Her boss sent her and a few other co-workers to the first True Identity Retreat. She did not want to be there. She sat with her table group and did not say a word or write in her workbook, because she knew someone else "this would be good for," and had a wall around herself. She was sure that none of this was of any use to her. Why in the world did God bring her to this?

But on Sunday afternoon, God started to knock a few bricks out of her wall. When she heard us talk about being a Daughter of the King something pierced her heart. She'd never seen herself that way.

She left the retreat, still not having said anything, and started thinking back to all she'd heard and experienced. God began to show her how much He loved her and how He wanted to bring out the softer side in her, help her be "His" girl. He wanted her to delight in friendships with women, and told her that some day she would be ministering to women. Slowly the wall started to come down and God continued to do an amazing transformation in her life.

She has many girlfriends now, is more comfortable with girly things, and she radiates precious inner beauty, which has made her even more beautiful on the outside. And she has pink duct tape!

Moving Forward

Are you "knowing" but not "believing" something? What would help you move from knowing about something to believing it and acting on that belief?

"I must have the approval of others to feel good about myself." This was a lie I lived with for a good part of my life. I constantly wanted to be affirmed by others, told I looked nice, did a good job, was so talented, was a good wife, mother, etc. I knew that lie led to a deep-seated fear

of rejection, making me a people-pleaser, too sensitive to criticism, withdrawn to avoid disapproval, and fearful of being open and vulnerable.

Once I began to understand how to replace lies with God's truth, I began to counter this lie with the truth that I am totally accepted by God, and do not have to fear rejection. (Colossians 1:19-22) When this truth made it the eighteen inches from my head (knowledge) to my heart (spirit) and *I believed it*, I was free of the fear of rejection, more transparent and open. I relaxed around others, enjoyed friendships, and received criticism with the right heart.

Sydney told me at a True Identity Retreat that not until she really began to believe that she was God's precious daughter, did she find freedom to be all God designed and intended for her to be. She said, "I knew it for years, but until I *believed* it, there was no change."

Take some time and examine some of the books you've been carrying around in your backpack.* When you can see it laid out in this type of format it may help you see how to move forward from the lie to the truth. Ask God to help you know His truth to counter the lie and what the result will be from believing the truth. Use this example and walk yourself through this process with each lie you have believed.

When a lie is revealed, it's okay, and sometimes good, to go back and allow the emotions from the lie to surface, to acknowledge the hurt, and release it. But don't stay in the lie. Many get stuck there. They start reliving it all, get sucked back in and start over analyzing and wallowing in it again. They receive and believe the lie all over again. Acknowledge it, renounce it and move forward into truth.

Trust the Lord to take you through this process. Get help if you need it. Know that He loves you intensely and wants to set you free to walk in your TRUE identity in Him.

Refer to the "Belief Systems" chart in the resources section at the back of this book to help you gain insight as to how the lie is impacting your thinking, beliefs and behavior.

Before You Read On

1. How do you "take every thought captive to Christ?" And how does this help you renew your mind?

2. Is worry or fear a result of one of the bigger "books" in your backpack? What lies have led you to be fearful or worried?

3. How do we erase the lies written on our hearts?

4. How does knowing the truth set us free?

5. Why do we want to keep going back to the "captor?"

6. Take a minute and look at the Belief Systems Chart in the back of this book. Take one of the lies in your "backpack" and walk it through the 4 categories like the examples given on the chart.

7. Are you "knowing" but not "believing" something? What would help you move from knowing about something to believing it and acting on that belief?

SUGGESTED PRAYER

Dear Heavenly Father, please help me to be so saturated in your Word that I can unpack my "backpack" by countering every lie with your truth and leave them at the foot of the cross. I want to be loosed of the chains that keep me in bondages and move toward freedom in you. Bring to my mind anyone that has offended or hurt me and help me to choose to forgive them. Not to hold any grievances against them, but to pray for them and let go of the hurt they inflicted on me. Heal me as I continue to trust you and your plan for my life. In Jesus' name. ~ Amen

Every man should keep a
fair-sized cemetary in which to
bury the faults of his friends.

~Henry Ward Beecher

Chapter 10
The Lock on the Chains

God expects forgiven people to forgive others.

-Bruce Hebel

Are you hanging on to a grudge? Want revenge? Another huge barrier to freedom and healing is not forgiving those who hurt you and holding on to past hurts. It's the lock on the chains that keep us in bondage. For many it is the most difficult step to take toward lasting freedom and healing.

Shelly was having a hard time forgiving her father for abusing her as a child. She was growing bitter and starting to experience physical problems that she knew were related to this issue. She believed if she forgave her father it would be "letting him off the hook." But her father was getting older and she felt terrible that as a Christian she was harboring bad feelings and had a strained relationship with him.

I asked her what she thought forgiving someone meant. She said, "Letting go and acting like nothing ever happened." I explained, "Forgiving and forgetting are two different things. Forgiving is not forgetting. The pain will fade in time, but you will not forget. Forgiveness is a choice, and act of your will. If you wait to *feel* like forgiving you never will. The feelings will follow the action. Once you choose to forgive, as God requires us to forgive others as He has forgiven us, (Ephesians 4:25-32), you will be set free from the bondage of bitterness and begin to heal.

"Vengeance is mine," says the Lord (Romans 12:19). It is not our job to exact revenge or judgment. That's God's job. When we forgive we are setting *ourselves* free. We are no longer chained to our past and those who hurt us. We can't change or fix the past, but we don't have to stay bound to it or the people who hurt us. God will bring healing as you forgive, not the other way around.

"He's never said he was sorry," Shelly said. I encouraged her not to base her forgiveness on an apology from her father. He may never apologize. Jesus did not wait for others to apologize to him before he forgave them (Luke 23:34). We are *commanded* to forgive (Luke 6:36). I encouraged her to pray and ask God to help her *choose* to forgive her father, to give her HIS love for him, and to bring healing to the deep wounds caused by this situation. God knows how much you are hurting. Run to Him for comfort and healing, and let go of the one who wounded you to Him.

(Note: Forgiving does *not* mean you stay in the abuse. God does not tolerate sin and neither should you. Set healthy, scriptural boundaries and put a stop to further abuse. Talk with a pastor, counselor, or trusted friend to help you if needed.)

Forgiveness Is . . .

Remember that forgiveness is a choice, and act of your will. Ask the Lord to help you make the choice to forgive no matter how you may be feeling about a person or situation.

FORGIVENESS IS A COMMAND

Mark 11:25-26 - *"Whenever you stand praying, forgive, if you have anything against anyone, so that your Father who is in heaven will also forgive you your transgressions. But if you do not forgive, neither will your Father who is in heaven forgive your transgressions"* (NASB).

Thank God for first forgiving you as you forgive others.

FORGIVENESS IS NOT SEEKING VENGEANCE

Romans 12:19 - *"'Vengeance is mine, I will repay,' says the Lord."*

God will deal with the person. It is not our job to exact revenge or judgment. That's God's job.

FORGIVENESS IS NOT WAITING FOR OTHERS TO APOLOGIZE

Luke 23:34 - *"And Jesus said, 'Father, forgive them, for they know not what they do.'"*

Jesus did not wait for others to apologize to him before he forgave them. God will bring healing as you forgive, not the other way around.

FORGIVENESS IS SETTING OURSELVES FREE

We can't fix our past but we will no longer be chained to the past and those who hurt us. Forgiving is not holding on to the past hurt. You may never forget. The pain will fade in time, but every time you remember, you remind yourself that you have forgiven that person.

Freedom

I, too, struggled with forgiving those who had hurt me in the past. When I went through a "Freedom Appointment," part of Neil Anderson's Freedom in Christ ministries, I found major breakthroughs in this. As we went through the "7 Steps to Freedom," one of the steps is forgiveness. The woman taking me through the steps explained to me what forgiveness was and wasn't. I then prayed and asked God to bring to mind all the people I needed to forgive. I thought of some right away: my mother, my father, my brother, my grandmother, friends, and all the kids who had mocked and teased me. I prayed and chose to forgive each person on my list, then prayed that I would choose not to hold on to any resentment or right to seek revenge, and asked Him to heal my damaged emotions.

Then the woman asked if I wanted to release any angry thoughts against God. "God? I asked. "I don't have angry thoughts against God. I have a good relationship with God." But again as I thought about it, I did. I was angry that He allowed me to be born with a birth defect. I was disappointed that things didn't go the way I thought they should have, that I'd lost three children in miscarriage, and that He didn't heal me when I had prayed for it years ago. I prayed and released all these angry thoughts toward God and asked for His forgiveness.

At the end of this step I thanked God for setting me free from the bondage of bitterness and asked Him to bless those who had hurt me, in Jesus' name.

I had gone through a box of Kleenex and was exhausted, but I felt FREE after this step, and was so thankful that I could finally open the lock on the chains that had kept me in bondage for so many years!

Isaiah 61:1 – *"He has sent me to proclaim liberty to the captives, and the opening of the prison to those who are bound."* Pray and ask God to help you choose to forgive. Ask Him to give you HIS LOVE for the person who hurt you, and to bring healing to the deep wounds caused by the situation. God knows how much you are hurting. Run to Him for comfort and healing, pour your heart out to Him, and let go of the one who wounded you to Him. There is a saying, *"Unforgiveness is like drinking poison and expecting the other person to die."*

Jesus came to set His sons and daughters FREE! Break the lock on the chains and allow Him to heal you and set you free to be all He created you to be in your true identity in Him, where you can then allow others to be free to be who God made them to be. Cling to the promise that perfect love, His love, casts out all fear.

Before You Read On

1. What is forgiveness and what is it not?

2. Why is it important to forgive others? What happens when we don't forgive?

3. How does it help us to forgive others?

4. Ask the Lord to show you who you need to forgive and for what.

5. Is there anyone you are having difficulty forgiving? Pray the Lord will help you choose to forgive them and let go of the hurts they inflicted on you. Surrender them to the Lord and pray blessings on them.

SUGGESTED PRAYER

Dear Heavenly Father, bring to my mind anyone that has offended or hurt me and help me to choose to forgive them. Not to hold any grievances against them, but to pray for them and let go of the hurt they inflicted on me. Heal me as I continue to trust you and your plan for my life. In Jesus' name. ~ Amen

❀ ❀ ❀

Chapter 11
True Identity

You're a swan now!

When something is broken, who fixes it? If I have a broken watch, do I take it to a pilot to fix it? If I have a broken car, do I take it to a hairdresser? A broken arm to a chef? Of course not. Yet when we are reflecting from a "broken mirror," feeling damaged, inferior, or insecure, we keep going back to wrong sources to fix it. And we wonder why it doesn't work right or heal!

Who better to fix something than the one who created it?

"For God made man in His own image" (Genesis 9:6b).

Reflecting From God's Mirror

When we want to discover WHO and WHOSE we really are, God's beloved children, and be free to live out of our true purpose and identity, we need to look to the right source. *The One who created us.* We need to look into HIS mirror, His Word, the Bible, to get a proper reflection and view of ourselves. To see ourselves as GOD sees us. Just as when the Ugly Duckling saw his reflection in the lake for the first time, he saw who he *truly* was. A beautiful swan!

We are all ugly ducklings, lost in our sin and in bondage to lies, before we are forgiven and redeemed through Jesus. (Romans 3:23-24 – *"for all have sinned and fall short of the glory of God, and all are justified freely by his grace through the redemption that came by Christ Jesus"* NIV.) When Jesus died on the cross and took the penalty for our sins, it allowed us to be reconciled to God, washed clean, made righteous, holy, and blameless in His sight (Ephesians 1:4 – *"For he chose us in Him before the creation of the world to be holy and blameless in His sight"* NIV.). Made into beautiful, white, sanctified swans!

Let it be clear though, that we are only redeemed in Christ. In fact, our natural born identity is as a sinner, unworthy of Him because His holiness cannot look at sin. But once we are in Christ we are given our true identity in Him. Who He originally intentioned us to be. We are rid of the filthy rags and put on the beautiful robes of righteousness. Isaiah 61:10 - *"I delight greatly in the LORD; my soul rejoices in my God. For he has clothed me with garments of salvation and arrayed me in a robe of his righteousness, as a bridegroom adorns his head like a priest, and as a bride adorns herself with her jewels"* (NIV).

Remember that Satan wants to rob us of life, but Jesus came that we may have life and have it abundantly in our true identity in Him! (John 10:10 – *"The thief comes only to steal and kill and destroy. I came that they may have life and have it abundantly."*)

New Creation

Before Christ I was trying to fight off the world alone. God wrapped His love around me to save me, protect me, nurture me, and heal me, then send me out to do His ministry.

I'm sitting outside on a sunny spring day in the north Georgia mountains writing this, watching a beautiful monarch butterfly flittering around some flowers in front of the deck. I love butterflies. They remind me of God's promise in 2 Corinthians 5:17 that *"if anyone is in Christ, he is a new creation. The old has passed away; behold the new has come."*

We are butterflies. God takes us through a metamorphosis from caterpillar to butterfly. We come to Him as sinners, get wrapped up in God's transforming, redeeming love, and emerge a new creation in Him, forgiven and free.

God doesn't do a makeover, trying to make something old look new; He makes us completely new. (Mark 2:22 - *"And no one puts new wine into old wineskins; if he does, the wine will burst the skins, and the wine is destroyed, and so are the skins. But new wine is for fresh wineskins."*)

The old me was now gone (Romans 6:6 – *"We know that our old self was crucified with Him in order that the body of sin might be brought to nothing, so that we would no longer be enslaved to sin."* Ephesians 4:22 – *"to put off your old self, which belongs to your former manner of life and is corrupt through deceitful desires."*). I could be FREE in the "new" me (Swan) (Romans 6:7 – *"For one who has died has been set free from sin."* Ephesians 4:23-24- "And to be renewed in the spirit of your minds, and put* *on the new self, created after the likeness of God in true righteousness and holiness.").*

The journey of ugly duckling to swan took twenty-one years on the outside. That same journey took forty-five years on the inside. Understanding how God made me, that I was not a mistake, writing God's Word on my heart, knowing and *believing* how much HE loved me, countering and erasing the lies with His truth, letting go of the past, and rejoicing in all I was in Christ and He in me, was part of the process to being set free in my TRUE identity in Christ!

Firmly Rooted

"I'm so sorry, but he took his life," I said to the precious young woman who had become very dear to my family. Those were the most difficult words I have ever had to say. She instantly went into shock and started sobbing, crying, "No, no, no." I didn't know the right words to console her so I just held her and cried with her, praying and asking God to help me help her. Then all of a sudden she looked at me through frightened tears and asked, "Are the police going to come and get me? He said if he did this it would be all my fault and I would go to jail." My heart broke again. "Of course not. This is not your fault. He lied to you when he said that." She didn't believe me. She went into a panic. Not only from the shock of hearing that she had just lost her husband to suicide, but also because she thought she was going to go to jail. I assured her everything was going to be okay, that she would come and live with us and we would take care of her. God was going to help us all through this.

She had only been married four months and her husband was on a rapid downward spiral of addiction to pain medications after suffering a car accident. He became more and more irrational and started threatening to kill himself, telling her it would be her fault if he did. She had just moved here from another country to marry him and was unsure of the laws surrounding this type of issue. Although there were many who tried to help her husband, Satan had such a grip on him that he succumbed to the lies, taking his life, leaving a young, frightened wife alone with nothing.

I was greatly concerned for her and how all of this might impact her newfound faith and future. All I knew at the moment was that she was to come home and live with us and God would see us through. One day at a time.

Those next days didn't get any easier, but God had His hand on His precious daughter and carried her through that very traumatic storm. We loved her and cared for her, cried with her and tried to answer all her questions. Our daughters adopted her as a sister and before long she was part of our family.

In the months ahead, as I got to know her better and spent more time in conversation with her, I discovered that part of why she felt her husband's death was her fault was not only because he told her it would be, but because of her sinful past. She felt God was punishing her for the bad things she had done as a teen and young adult. She couldn't believe that God loved her enough to forgive her for those things.

She came to our women's Bible study and was astonished that what we studied each week was exactly what she needed to learn about God and her relationship with Him. She would get so excited on the ride home, saying to me, "Mom Jen, wasn't that cool how we are studying about God's forgiveness this week? God knew I needed that right now!" My heart soared. God was wooing her and affirming her in her identity in Him.

She was more firmly rooted in God's Word and healing, and by the time she went back to her country, she knew her TRUE Identity in Christ. She was set free like a butterfly to pursue all God had planned for her, plans for a future and hope, a new creation in Him.

WHO and WHOSE

We all need to know WHO and WHOSE we are in Christ and who Christ is IN US. Read through the first four chapters of Ephesians. It is rich with promises and descriptions of who we are in Christ and who He is in us:

Holy and blameless before Him (1:4)

Adopted by Him (1:5)

Redeemed through Him (1:7)

Forgiven (1:7)

Can know Him and His will (1:9)

Sealed with the promise of the Holy Spirit (1:13)

Made us alive in Christ, Saved (2:5)

His workmanship (2:10)

Reconciled to God (2:16)

Access to the Father (2:18)

Able to do far more abundantly than we ask or think (3:20)

Created after the likeness of God in true righteousness and holiness (4:24)

Who we are in Him helps us to be set free from the condemnation of sin to be all He designed and desires for us to be, and understanding who He is IN US, helps us to do the work He has called and equipped us to do (make disciples of all nations) and walk free in our True Identity in Him.

A woman I worked with told me that she was feeling better about herself since she had gotten some self-esteem. I asked her how she had obtained this self-esteem, wondering if she got it in the cereal aisle at the grocery store as she made it sound. She said she had gone to a psychologist who taught her how to tell herself positive things, including standing in front of a mirror each morning and telling herself she was beautiful, powerful, in charge of her own destiny, and in control. A few months later I asked her if it was still working and she said, "Not so much." She was slipping back into depression.

The problem is not low self-esteem; *it is not esteeming Christ in us.* We were created to be only satisfied in Him. When we try to feel better about ourselves from our own sinful self, it will always be a fleeting, empty thing. Since there is no good thing in us, (Mark 10:18 *"Why do you call me good?" Jesus answered. "No one is good—except God alone"* (NIV), it cannot come from within us. When we become Christians, Christ gives us the gift of the Holy Spirit (Acts 2:38 – *"Peter replied, 'Repent and be baptized, every one of you, in the name of Jesus Christ for the forgiveness of your sins. And you will receive the gift of the Holy Spirit'"* NIV.). We now have Christ living IN US. It is Christ in us who gives us life, hope, purpose, fulfillment, and all we need to walk through life in victory. (Romans 8:9 –*"But you are not living the life of the flesh, you are living the life of the Spirit, if the [Holy] Spirit of God [really] dwells within you [directs and controls you]. But if anyone does not possess the [Holy] Spirit of Christ, he is none of His [he does not belong to Christ, is not truly a child of God]"* AMP.) Having a healthy self-esteem is a by-product of esteeming Christ in us. Our identity is no longer what happened to us as a child and young adult, but what happened IN us through Christ.

Understanding who I am in Christ and who He is in me can be confusing. Picture it like this. You have three envelopes. On the front of one, write GOD. The second, HOLY SPIRIT, and third, ME. Now put the envelope with HOLY SPIRIT written on it inside the envelope with ME written on it. Then put the envelope with ME written on it inside the one with GOD written on it. We have our TRUE identity in God (ME inside the GOD envelope) and at the same time have Him living inside of us, (the HOLY SPIRIT envelope inside the ME envelope).

Many of us Christians do not live like we have the mighty power of God (Holy Spirit) living in us. I didn't for a long time. I knew that I had the gift of the Holy Spirit in me upon confession of faith in Jesus Christ and then baptism, but I was not allowing Him to have permeating influence on me. I still struggled with worry, fear, depression, and insecurities, but I didn't need more of the Holy Spirit; I needed to let Him have more of me. I was walking in the flesh much more than I was walking in the Spirit. (Galatians 5:16 – *"But I say, walk and live [habitually] in the [Holy] Spirit [responsive to and controlled and guided by the Spirit]; then you will certainly not gratify the cravings and desires of the flesh (of human nature without God)"* (NIV.). No wonder I felt defeated and beaten down a lot of the time, trudging around with that heavy backpack on saying, "Yeah, I'm a Christian. Can't you tell? See how happy and joyful I am?"Life is often very difficult and challenging, but we are ones who have the living God dwelling inside of us and we must also show that on the outside.

Believing WHO WE ARE in Christ destroys feelings of INFERIORITY

Believing WHERE WE ARE in Christ destroys feelings of INSECURITY

Believing WHO CHRIST IS IN US destroys feelings of INADEQUACY

We have been given all we need in Christ to live a fulfilled and victorious life! (Romans 8:37 – *"In all these things we are more than conquerors through Him who loved us."*) Now we need to believe it and engage in it!

Before You Read On

1. Has there been a battle within you between your "old self" (Ugly Duckling) and "new self" (Swan)? Do you still see yourself as an ugly duckling or as a swan?

2. What does walking in the flesh look like to you and walking in the Spirit look like?

3. What does it mean to be "a new creation in Christ?" How should that affect our behavior?

4. What is the difference in WHO we are in Christ and who He is IN US?

5. How does knowing your TRUE identity in Christ change the way you see yourself? How can it impact the core of your being and outlook on life?

6. What steps can you take to allow the Holy Spirit to have a more permeating influence on you?

SUGGESTED PRAYER

Dear Heavenly Father, thank you that I am a new creation in you! Thank you that the "old self" is dead and I am now fully alive in You. Remind me each day of all I am in You and who You are in me. Help me to embrace and stand firm in my TRUE identity and allow it to transform me from the inside out. In Jesus' name ~ Amen

Wedding day 1986.   *Celebrating our 25th wedding anniversary in 2011.*

Chapter 12
Uniquely You

Lord, let me be in the total creation you have made me to be. Not to be squeezed into someone else's mold, but to allow your grace & plan to take its work in me.

Fearfully And Wonderfully Made

"For you created my inmost being, you knit me together in my mother's womb. I praise you because I am fearfully and wonderfully made; your works are wonderful, I know that full well. My frame was not hidden from you when I was made in the secret place. When I was woven together in the depths of the earth. Your eyes saw my unformed body. All the days ordained for me were written in your book before one of them came to be." Psalm 139:13-16 (NIV).

Part of God's "knitting together" was giving us a specific personality type. We were born with our personality. It doesn't change. How it manifests itself may change, but our core personality type does not. How God "wired us" is a significant part of our identity.

In one college sculpting class, we were to sculpt a head, or bust as the artsy types call it, and had to choose the best kind of clay for this assignment. Our instructor explained the importance of using clay that is pliable, not too soft, would hold its shape, but not dry out too quickly. I chose my block of clay, put it on the sculpting stand and began to carve, shape and sculpt a head form out of it. I could sculpt and mold the clay to the shape of a head, an animal, a building, a plant, whatever I desired. But whatever shape it took, it would still be made of clay. The clay did not change, the shape did.

It's the same with our personalities. We are born with a particular personality or personality blend (the clay) that does not change. However, just like my example of sculpting, circumstances in which you live and grow up, your family, outside influences, God can all be part of the "shaping" of your character.

Decisions, Decisions, Decisions

I wonder what to wear today?

Every morning I would stand in my closet and ask myself that question. It drove me nuts. Why do I have such a hard time making decisions? Why am I such a perfectionist? Why is everyone always in such a hurry, and why can't everyone get along?

I really struggled with these things in myself until I first heard about the four personality types, Sanguine (wants fun), Choleric (wants control), Phlegmatic (wants peace), Melancholic (wants perfection), from Florence

Littauer when she spoke at a Billy Graham luncheon in 1983. I was fascinated. I later bought her book, *Personality Plus*, and ate it up. For the first time in my life I was beginning to understand why as a Phlegmatic I did things the way I did. Why I thought about things the way I did. Why I communicated the way I did. Why I hated conflict so much and had such a hard time making decisions. What sort of situations stress me out. The light bulb went on! I wasn't crazy after all.

The biggest impact of knowing the personality types was when I married a Dutchman. For quite a while I wasn't sure what was cultural and what was personality. I spent twenty months living in Amsterdam, where I met and married my husband, and had the opportunity to get to know a bit about the Dutch culture as well as spend time with my husband's family. I thought all Dutch were like my husband and his family. Not until my husband and I took a personality profile survey together several years later, did I begin to sort out what was Dutch and what was my husband's personality type—Choleric.

It also greatly helped us to understand one another better, be patient with one another's weaknesses and encourage one another's strengths. It has saved many possible disagreements and has smoothed the way for us to learn to communicate and resolve conflict in a healthy way. We focus more on being a united team, knowing God put us two "opposites" together to complement one another and be stronger. We kept Christ in the center, and stopped trying to change one another. Only God can do that!

Uniquely You

Understanding more about your own personality type and that of others will help you better recognize that others are not "wrong" because they are different from you, they are just different. God made us all unique to work together as diverse parts of the "body" of Christ (1 Corinthians 12:24-27). There is no other "you" in the entire universe. Finding contentment with the personality type that God has given you is an important step in understanding how God knit you together and rejoicing in it! Not wishing you had someone else's personality type, but accepting that God knew just the perfect personality type for you and how you can grow in Christ-like character in it.

Why Can't Everyone Just Get Along?

"Behold, how good and pleasant it is when brothers dwell in unity" – Psalm 133:1

We have all four personality types in our family. My husband is primarily Choleric, I am Phlegmatic, my older daughter is Melancholic, and my younger daughter is Sanguine. It makes for some very interesting dynamics! But as the girls have grown up with an understanding of their own personality type, each other's, and ours as their parents, they too have learned to encourage one another's strengths and have patience with one another's weaknesses. Knowing about the personality types has improved the relationships within our family and helped with relationships outside our family.

Being aware of the personalities of your parents, siblings, children, co-workers, schoolmates, boss, pastor, small group, and others you are in contact with on a regular basis can greatly enhance and improve those relationships. God tells us in the Bible that it is our aim to strive to get along with everyone when it is in our power to do so. Romans 12:18 tells us – *"If possible, so far as it depends on you, live peaceably with all,"* and in John 13:34-35 – *"A new commandment I give to you, that you love one another; just as I have loved you, you also are to love one another. By this all people will know that you are my disciples, if you have love for one another."* Understanding how God made each of us in a key tool to achieve this.

One Kenyan woman emailed me after attending the True Identity Retreat in Kenya that once she understood her personality and that of her husband and children, along with the rest of the True Identity message, her family relationships drastically improved. She said she didn't argue with her husband anymore and she began to encourage him and help support the emotional needs of his personality. She knew how to better love, motivate, and affirm her children. She felt knowing this material has now helped her entire family be set free to be who God designed them to be! On my second trip to Kenya in November 2012, this was confirmed again by many who had been a part of the first True Identity Retreat, sharing with me that understanding personalities and the True Identity message was bringing a new unity to their families, churches, and communities!

Tapestry Of Love

Picture of all of us as a tapestry God is weaving. We are each individual colored threads God is lovingly weaving together into the Body of Christ. When you look at the back of the tapestry, it is a mess! Threads going every which way, knots, clumps of threads together, threads sticking out. But when you turn it over you see each thread perfectly intertwined with the rest, displaying a masterpiece on the finished side.

As I have been working with the personality concepts for over twenty-five years now, I have seen how significant it has been for others to understand how God made them. It has brought new freedom in their relationship with themselves, God, and those they interact with. This is a primary reason why this is included in the True Identity teaching, to help others better understand this part of their identity. I hope you will discover the same for yourself. It is an important piece of our True Identity!

Before You Read On

1. What is your personality (clay) type? How does knowing this help you better understand yourself and how God made you?

2. Read Ephesians 2:10. Write down 5 personality strengths—your positive attributes—that you enjoy exhibiting and using to bless others.

3. Read Psalm 139:23-24 and Isaiah 64:8. List some of the weaknesses you feel you struggle with. Ask the Lord to begin to help you transform them into strengths.

4. How does understanding your personality type and that of others help set you free in your relationship with yourself, God, and with others?

SUGGESTED PRAYER

Heavenly Father, thank you that before I was formed in the womb, You had me in mind and created me just as I am. Help me to see the way you shaped, formed, and made me is perfect in your sight. You gave me a unique personality and distinctive physical traits. Help me to delight in and accept my uniqueness and realize the wonderful truth that I am unlike anyone else You ever made! Help me to also be open to how You may desire to change my weaknesses into strengths and to continue to strive to be more like You, and to remember that I honor You in being all that You created me to be! In Jesus' name ~ Amen.

For more detail information and understanding of the four personality types, I would recommend Maritta Littauer's book, *Wired That Way*. A personality profile is in the back of the book for you to fill in and find out which type/blend you are.

With my beautiful daughters Carina and Sophia.

Chapter 13
Daughter of the King

Jesus came to announce to us that an identity based on success, popularity, and power is a false identity—an illusion! Loudly and clearly he says; You are not what the world makes you, but you are children of God.

-Henri Nouwen

"Mirror, mirror on the wall. Who's the fairest of them all?" The evil queen in the story Snow White asks daily, hoping the mirror will tell her it is she. And just like the queen, every woman wants to be beautiful, to know she is lovely and valued.

True Beauty

1 Peter 3:4 tells us, *"But let your adorning be the hidden person of the heart with the imperishable beauty of a gentle and quiet spirit, which in God's sight is very precious."*

Staci Eldridge says it well in her book, *Captivating*: "A woman of true beauty is a woman who in the depths of her soul is at rest, trusting God because she has come to know Him to be worthy of her trust. She exudes a sense of calm, a sense of rest, and invites those around her to rest as well."

As Daughters of the King, we are truly beautiful not only because that is how God sees us, but because we have Christ in us. He radiates from within and makes us not only beautiful on the inside, but even more beautiful on the outside. God showed me this as I went through years of reconstructive surgery, dental procedures, weight struggles, and feeling judged for what I looked like. The more intimate I grew in my relationship with Him, the more I saw myself as He sees me. Every time I had a negative thought about myself, the Lord would remind me how HE saw me. Every time someone said something cruel, the Lord was right there to comfort me with HIS perspective and thoughts toward me. As He continued to heal deep wounds with His truth and unconditional love, I was able to rest in the peace and beauty that He had placed deep within me.

"But the LORD said to Samuel, 'Do not consider his appearance or his height, for I have rejected him. The LORD does not look at the things man looks at. People look at the outward appearance, but the LORD looks at the heart.'" 1 Samuel 16:7 (NIV).

Precious In His Sight

A woman asked the crowd if someone had a twenty-dollar bill she could borrow. She promised she would give it back. She took the bill and started crumpling it up. She crumpled it as tight as she could, tossed it on the ground, and stomped on it. The donor was getting a bit nervous. She picked it up and asked the crowd if anyone wanted it. Everyone's hand went up. No matter how much it was folded, crumpled, or stomped on, it had not lost its value. It was still worth twenty-dollars.

The same is for us. No matter how much we are crumpled up, abused, soiled and stomped on in life, we are still of great value to God. The things that have happened to us do not determine or take away our value. As Isaiah 43:1-5 says, we are precious in His eyes.

"But now thus says the Lord, he who created you, O Jacob, he who formed you, O Israel: 'Fear not, for I have redeemed you; I have called you by name, you are mine. When you pass through the waters, I will be with you; and through the rivers, they shall not overwhelm you; when you walk through fire you shall not be burned, and the flame shall not consume you. For I am the LORD your God, the Holy One of Israel, your Savior. I give Egypt as your ransom, Cush and Seba in exchange for you. Because you are precious in my eyes, and honored, and I love you.'"

Stenitta never thought she was beautiful. Growing up, people would say that her sister was beautiful and she was smart. She always wanted to be thought of as beautiful like her sister. And her sister always wanted to be thought of as smart like her. Because of what someone had repeatedly said to her, she went through life until her mid thirties thinking that she was of no value to God and others because she thought she was not beautiful.

She attended a special prayer time with a group of fellow believers and someone prayed for her saying, *"God wants you to know how beautiful you are to Him. How much He loves you and values you. You are precious in His sight!"* She started to cry and felt set free from the lie that she was not beautiful and therefore was of no value to God and others. It changed her life!

I've heard a similar story from countless women. They have felt ugly, worthless, unforgivable, filthy, guilty, unlovable, and broken. We need to know and believe how much GOD loves us and values us. Enough that He sent His son to die for our sins and reconcile us to a right relationship with Himself (John 3:16), for it is only through Christ in us that He sees us as perfect. All of this should mean so much more than what others think of us. Believe me, I was one of those women and I allowed others and the world to determine my beauty and value. I headed for the pit of despair with a sense of no way out. And there would not have been if not for God breaking in and showing me how much HE loves and values me, and me believing and embracing it!

Royalty

I love the biblical story of Esther. King Ahasuerus once summoned Queen Vashti to come before him and she refused. She was told that she was never again to come before King Ahasuerus, and that the king was going to give her royal position to another who was better than she (Esther 1:19b). The king appointed officers to gather all the beautiful young virgins to the king's harem. He told them to give the women cosmetics and *"let the young woman who pleases the king be queen instead of Vashti"* (Esther 2:4). Esther, a beautiful, young, orphaned Jew who was being raised by her uncle, Mordecai, was taken into the king's palace. It was customary for women of the harem to spend twelve months beautifying themselves to have one night with the king. If the king was pleased and asked for her by name, she could return to him.

When it came Esther's turn, *"The king loved Esther more than all the women, and she won grace and favor in his sight more than all the virgins, so that he set the royal crown on her head and made her queen instead of Vashti"* (Esther 2:17), which eventually led to the saving of her people, the Jews.

One year to prepare for one night with a king!

God is our Father and loves us dearly as his children. 2 Corinthians 6:18 tells us, *"And I will be a father to you, and you shall be sons and daughters to me, says the Lord Almighty."* and John 1:12-13, *"But to all who did receive Him, who believed in the name, he gave the right to become children of God, who were born, not of blood nor of the will of the flesh nor of the will of man, but of God."*

Because we are sons and daughters of the King, this makes us royalty!

Isaiah 62:3 reminds us, *"You will be a crown of splendor in the Lord's hand, a royal diadem in the hand of your God"* (NIV).

Esther took one year to prepare for one night with a King. God is giving us a lifetime to prepare for an eternity with Him, *THE* King!

A beautiful example of how knowing we are royalty can profoundly transform us happened when I was in Kenya taking a group of Kenyan women ministry leaders through a True Identity Retreat. On Sunday morning when we told them about being a Daughter of the King, royalty, one woman said, "No one has ever told us this before. Is it really true?" I shared the scriptures above, so they could underline it in their Bibles and go back to it and be reminded of it over and over again.

You see, women in Kenya are often treated like property. They live very difficult lives with no rights and feel they are of little value other than being workhorses all day long. They are the ones who haul heavy water jugs up from the stream or wells, gather wood for cooking, prepare all the meals, clean, and take care of the children. They do not have all the modern conveniences we have, or all the privileges of women in more developed countries. It is also common practice for husbands to beat their wives. Some women even believe that if their husbands do not beat them, they do not really love them.

So when these women heard they are Daughters of the King, princesses, their entire countenance changed! They started introducing themselves as "Princess so and so" and dancing and celebrating. They were beaming with joy! One woman said, "It doesn't matter what anyone says about me now. I know I am God's princess and I am beautiful and special in His sight." Another said, "I am so beautiful in God's eyes I could win any beauty contest!" My heart soared as I saw these women embrace their TRUE identity as precious, beautiful Daughters of the King!

Kingdom Identity

Your true identity is really your Kingdom Identity. We are told in John 8:23, *"But he continued, 'You are from below; I am from above. You are of this world; I am not of this world'"* (NIV). And in John 18:36, *"Jesus said, 'My kingdom is not of this world. If it were, my servants would fight to prevent my arrest by the Jewish leaders. But now my kingdom is from another place'"* (NIV).

As God revealed my true identity, my kingdom identity, he gave me a picture of a huge, filthy trash heap. Gaunt, ragged people frantically dug through the trash trying to find food and something of sustenance. I was at the edge of the trash heap, trying to find things of value. God spoke to me and said, "Why are you still digging around in the trash heap when you should be at the palace? You were made to live in the palace. Stop going back to the trash heap." It struck me that every time I believed a lie or didn't see myself as God saw me, I was going back to the trash heap (the world) and trying to find my value there, when God designed me to live as His princess in the palace. A place, where because I have trusted in and been redeemed through Christ, He sees me as beautiful, priceless, of great value, righteous, blameless, forgiven, and free. Where I have the healthy food and sustenance in Him. I need to live in my kingdom identity, not my earthly one. I am in this world but not of this world. (John 17:15 – *"Do not ask that you take them out of the world, but that you keep them from the evil one. They are not of this world, just as I am not of the world."*) My citizenship is in Heaven. (Philippians 3:20 – *"But our citizenship is in heaven. And we eagerly await a Savior from there, the Lord Jesus Christ."*)

Any time one of my daughters asks me, "Do you think I'm pretty?" I resoundingly say, "Yes!" I see the beauty God has placed inside and out. It breaks my heart that they don't see it and believe it. It must break God's heart ten times more when we, His creation, don't see it. When we are unhappy with how He made us, we are saying He made a mistake. We feel it's a mistake because we may not look, or be like what the world says we should. Not God. Through our trust and redemption in Christ, we are beautiful and lovely in His eyes. Fearfully and wonderfully made (Psalm 139:14).

God wants to affirm in you that you are HIS princess. You are royalty. Precious, worthy, cherished, and greatly loved! Reflecting HIS glory!

Picture yourself walking down a red carpet with a beautifully decorated mirror at the end of it. You see the reflection of a princess in the mirror. God is standing by that mirror with a smile and outstretched arms. As you reach Him, He lovingly wraps you in a comforting hug. You feel unconditionally and completely loved. He then places a magnificent crown on your head and tells you, "My child, you are my beautiful, precious daughter. I love you."

The Ultimate Love Letter

I remember when my husband and I started dating in Amsterdam; we would send each other special notes and love letters. I loved going to the mailbox and finding a letter from my special someone. My heart would quicken as I opened it, knowing his letters always made me feel beautiful, cherished, and loved.

There is another love letter I received, and continue to receive daily, that reassures me that I am redeemed, beautiful, loved, and cherished by the One who knows me best. Knows just what encouragement I need, what exhortation, redirection and guidance, affirmation, praise, truth. It is a love letter from God. The Bible is God's love letter to us.

From *The Father's Love Letter,* all from scripture:

My Precious Child,

You may not know me, but I KNOW EVERYTHING ABOUT YOU. I know when you sit down and when you rise up. Even the HAIRS ON YOUR HEAD ARE NUMBERED. For you were MADE IN MY IMAGE. In me you LIVE and MOVE and HAVE YOUR BEING. For you are my OFFSPRING. I knew you even before you were conceived. YOU WERE NOT A MISTAKE, for all your days are WRITTEN IN MY BOOK. You are FEARFULLY and WONDERFULLY MADE. I knit you together in your mother's womb. And brought you forth on the day you were born.

I have been misrepresented by those that don't know me. I am NOT DISTANT and angry, but am the COMPLETE EXPRESSION OF LOVE. And it is my desire to LAVISH MY LOVE ON YOU. Simply because YOU ARE MY CHILD and I am your Father. I offer you more than your earthly father ever could, for I AM THE PERFECT FATHER.

Every GOOD GIFT that you receive COMES FROM MY HAND. For I am your PROVIDER and I MEET ALL YOUR NEEDS. My plan for your future has always been filled with HOPE, because I love you with an EVERLASTING LOVE. My thoughts toward you are countless as the sand on the sea-shore, and I REJOICE OVER YOU with singing. I will NEVER STOP DOING GOOD FOR YOU, for you are my TREASURED POSSESSION.

I desire to ESTABLISH YOU with ALL MY HEART and with ALL MY SOUL. I want to show you GREAT and MARVELOUS THINGS. If you SEEK ME with all your heart, you will FIND ME. I am able to do more for you than you could possibly imagine.

I am the GREATEST ENCOURAGER and I am also the Father who COMFORTS you in all your troubles. When you are brokenhearted, I am CLOSE TO YOU. As a shepherd carries a lamb, I have CARRIED YOU CLOSE TO MY HEART. One day I will WIPE AWAY EVERY TEAR from your eyes. And I'll TAKE AWAY ALL THE PAIN you have suffered on this earth.

I am your Father, and I LOVE YOU even as I love my son, Jesus. For in JESUS, my LOVE for you is REVEALED. He came to demonstrate that I AM FOR YOU, not against you. And to tell you that I AM NOT COUNTING YOUR SINS. Jesus died so that YOU and I COULD BE TOGETHER. His death was the ULTIMATE EXPRESSION of MY LOVE FOR YOU. I gave up everything I loved that I might gain your love. And NOTHING will SEPARATE YOU FROM MY LOVE again. COME HOME and I'll throw the biggest party heaven has ever seen. I have ALWAYS BEEN FATHER.

I am WAITING FOR YOU.

You are LOVED...

You are FORGIVEN...

You are PRECIOUS ... and YOU ARE MINE!

Your Loving Father, GOD

Remember, your TRUE identity is as a daughter of THE King. He wants to show you off, take you to the ball and dance with you. Celebrate a free and abundant life with you! Take that backpack off and go get your dancing shoes!

Before You Read On

1. How would you define beautiful? What is true beauty to you?

2. Have you trusted in and been redeemed in Christ? Do you see yourself as God's child? Do you know deep down inside how much He loves you? If not, what is keeping you from embracing that truth? Pray right now that He will solidify His love for you in your heart and free you from anything that is keeping you from believing it.

3. How does knowing WHO and WHOSE you TRULY ARE as a Daughter of the King, change

how you see yourself and impact the way you live your life?

4. What part of the "Father's Love Letter" especially speaks to you? Why?

5. Take a moment and in the back of this book write Truths that counter the lies you have believed and about who you are in Christ on the page with the mirror drawing.

SUGGESTED PRAYER

Dear Heavenly Father, I praise you that I am a "Crown of splendor in your hand," precious in your sight, beautiful, cherished and your princess. Continue to mold me and shape me into Christ-likeness; to be beautiful from the inside out. Free me from anything that is holding me back from embracing your truth and love. Help me to walk confidently each knowing I am your treasured child! In Jesus' name. ~ Amen.

Chapter 14
Embracing Your True Identity

*I want to go deeper with God and learn to
walk wholly in TRUTH in Him, and I pray
I can inspire others to do the same.*

The more we fall in love with Jesus, the less we will think about ourselves. When we focus on Him, He fills us up, gives us purpose, and a proper perspective, deep joy, and love for others. He helps us to see the world through *His* eyes. When we know how much He loves us, who we are in Him, that we are secure in Him, and we no longer need to try to manipulate people, judge them, or cut them down to feel better about ourselves. We can rejoice in who God made them to be. We can encourage people, be genuinely happy for the things God is doing in their lives, be ourselves around them, forgive them, and build them up. Forgiveness brings freedom, which produces free relationships.

"I am my own worst enemy," my daughter would say to me. She hated that she would get self absorbed and hard on herself. When she didn't measure up she would verbally tear herself apart. She'd had her share of battles through puberty and teen years, suffered a lot of rejection, and struggled to come to peace with her body and personality.

We moved a lot during her childhood years, and she always felt like the "new kid on the block," not quite fitting in. Just when she would make new friends we would move or she would go to a new school. She always felt like she was on the outside looking in. She would try harder and harder to prove herself to others, wanting to be the best and be noticed. She disliked those things about herself and just wanted to be free from the "me" in her.

She's discovering the unique and special qualities God has woven into her life as a result of all she's been through. He is preparing her for His purposes in her life and is learning to let go of her past and trust Him to bring healing and confidence in who He made her to be. She, too, is becoming a beautiful swan.

Redeemed Relationships

A lot of dysfunction can happen in families when God is not at the center, when relationships are operating from a sinful, selfish, broken place instead of out of freedom in Christ. My family was no exception. Although my mother took us three kids to church, and I am thankful for a Godly foundation in my life, I grew up in a *religious home*, not a *Christ-centered home*. We were all operating out of worldly thoughts, actions, bondages and strongholds.

My father, trapped in the lie of the "American Dream," was a workaholic seeking to become one of the elite in our town, gripped by pornography, and emotionally distant. My mother's identity was wrapped up in maintaining her beauty, (which was magnified by my father's pornography addiction) and being a totally devoted mother. She became lonely as we grew more independent and went off to college. She turned to alcohol to numb her pain. My older brother craved my father's approval and tried to gain it through striving to be the best at sports, school and work, the same as our father had in life. He turned to substances to numb his pain and sense of rejection. My younger brother was well liked by everyone and was the "golden child" of our family. But he, too, was craving our father's approval and chased hard after the same "American Dream," thinking it would win our father's admiration and bring fulfillment. Two years after my mother died, my father remarried and his new bride came with her own dysfunctional baggage that deeply impacted both of our families. As my brothers and I got married, those relationships then added more to the family dynamics and dysfunction. We really were a sorry, messed up bunch!

As radio host Paul Harvey used to say, I want to share, "the rest of the story" because we serve a mighty, loving God and He alone can rescue us from ourselves and our sin-filled bondages and strongholds and redeem relationships.

God rescued me first in our family. As I grew in my faith and understanding of Christ's sanctifying work in my own life, along with embracing the power of prayer, forgiveness, and true identity in Christ, I began to pray for my family to come to salvation and also be set free from the bondages and strongholds they were locked in to, and that the relationship I had with each one would be healed and restored.

One by one God miraculously redeemed each one of these relationships! God allowed me to live at home the last nine months of my mother's life, giving us many special days together reading God's Word, sharing about Christ and talking about heaven. I saw my mother let go of years of guilt and depression and embrace the hope of heaven.

After my mother's passing, through shared grief, my father and I drew much closer. I also let go of years of unmet expectations and forgave my father for many hurts. As he was searching for God in the twilight years of his life, I was able to lovingly witness to him and lead him to Christ two weeks before he passed away. As we read and prayed through Romans 10:9, (*if you confess with your mouth that Jesus is Lord and believe in your heart that God raised him from the dead, you will be saved*) he asked Jesus to be Lord and Savior of his life. He said later that evening that he felt a peace he had never felt before. He was no longer afraid of dying.

I couldn't believe after almost thirty-five years of praying I was now having deep, Christ-centered conversations with my brothers! The relationship with my older brother was healed through forgiveness and a new relationship as brother and sister in Christ. We now have a genuine love and concern for one another, pray for one another and love the times we can be together. I was always close to my younger brother, but now we have an even greater connection through our shared love for the Lord. All three of us are in some type of ministry work today!

God redeemed the deeply fractured relationship with my stepmother after many years of misunderstanding and a season of not speaking to one another for four years.

Through God pouring *His* love for my stepmother out through me, walls of bitterness came crumbling down, and a new, loving relationship was established. We now often talk on the phone and always end our conversations with, "I love you!"

Not only did He redeem family relationships, but as I was freed of "me" in relationships God has blessed me with numerous special friendships over the years, after spending so many years alone and lonely. I feel God has graciously fulfilled the promise of Joel 2:25, *"I will restore to you the years that the swarming locusts has eaten,"* in my life!

Upward And Outward Focus

The other wonderful thing that happens when we embrace our true identity in Christ is that we can be healed and set free from a self absorbed, inward focus, to an upward and outward focus as Jesus commanded us to do. (Luke 10:27 – *"Love your neighbor as yourself"* NIV.) When we are constantly engrossed in our own problems and locked in a "woe is me" attitude, we are not free to be about God's kingdom business. We are too busy thinking about ourselves to have any time to think about God, much less other people. We feel "It's all about me. Look out for number one."

There is great joy and fulfillment that comes in helping others come to understand how much God loves them and desires to call them His own. We can be free to help take care of their physical needs, but even more importantly their spiritual needs. It's not about us anymore; it's all about HIM and having our purpose and identity in Him! As John Piper says, "God is most glorified when we are most satisfied in Him."

When I embraced my True Identity in Christ and *really believed it*, I recognized that I am not worthy apart from my life in Him. I was released from the chains of pride, looking for approval from others, fear of rejection, and worry. I grew to be happy and accepting of how God made me, knowing it was with great purpose and not a mistake. I was able to trust God securely knowing that He would give me all I needed to step outside my comfort zones and do all He was calling me to do. I rejoice that I am now open to go wherever God takes me to share with others around the globe how embrace *their* true identity in Christ! When I look in the mirror I still see the scar, but now it is a reminder of HIS scars and how much He loves me, and the price He paid so I could live in eternity with Him. I don't see the ugly duckling I see a swan. A sanctified swan! I am ALIVE, LOVED, FORGIVEN, HEALED, and FREE!

Before You Read On

1. How does fully embracing our true identity in Christ change our view of others and ourselves?

2. How does being free of "me" help me be free in my relationship with others?

3. What things can you do to have more of an upward and outward focus? Who around you can you help today?

4. Can you tell a story of how God redeemed a relationship in your life?

5. Pray for relationships in your life that need to be redeemed and trust God to do a mighty work in each one. Ask God to give you all you need to do your part in the work He has to bring reconciliation and healing.

SUGGESTED PRAYER

Dear Heavenly Father, help me to fully embrace my true identity in You, trusting you to help me "get over myself" and be free to be all you have created and designed for me to be. Help me to focus on You, delight in the work You have for me to do and be more aware of the needs of those around me. Thank you Lord, that in you I am fully alive, loved, forgiven, healed, and FREE in my TRUE identity! In Jesus' name ~ Amen

Jesus first, others next,
and yourself last
spells J-O-Y!

~ **Linda Byler,** *Running Around (And Such)*

Chapter 15
Walking In Your True Identity

The level of success of walking in freedom in your true identity is dependent on the level of intimacy in your relationship with Christ.

The day after the ball, your elegant gown is hung back up in the closet, your sweats are comfortably back on, and you are facing a day of the same old routine. The memories from an enchanted evening fade quickly as you change a diaper and clean the dishes. Often after we've experienced a mountaintop high with God and have broken chains of bondage, we are easily sucked back into everyday routine and find ourselves returning to old thought patterns and habits. Hearing and receiving the same old lies. Putting the backpacks on again. The enemy is going to do all he can to convince you that your freedom is just temporary, and God's Word is not really true. Walking in your true identity and remaining free in Christ can be a challenge. Difficult, but possible.

Wind Up Versus Plug In

When I was young, wind-up toys were very popular. I had a little car that I would wind up, put on the ground, release, and watch race across the room until it slowly ran out of "gas" and stopped. I would wind it up and do the whole thing over and over again.

Compare that wind-up toy with a plug-in toy. You plug it in, turn it on and it will run as long as there is continuous power. You can play for hours, days if you want to, not having to stop and crank up the power again.

Walking in your true identity can be like the wind up toy. We wind ourselves up, "FAITH, FAITH, FAITH, FAITH", and as the day wears on and difficult things are bombarding our day, "faith, faith, faith, faith." Your faith dwindles and runs out. Worry and fear start to creep back in. We wind ourselves up each day and go out into the world in our own strength, and we run out of steam. We feel discouraged and feel defeated. We are slipping back into the pit.

We need to plug in to a continuous power source.

John 15:4-5 tells us, *"Abide in me, and I in you. As the branch cannot bear fruit by itself, unless it abides in the vine, neither can you, unless you abide in me. I am the vine; you are the branches. Whoever abides in me and I in him, he it is that bears much fruit, for apart from me you can do nothing."* We don't have to manufacture the source of power ourselves. All we need to do is ABIDE (plug in) in Christ (be a branch). The power comes through Him, the vine, to us. If the branch is cut off from the vine, it withers and dies. When we cut ourselves off from God, we will wither and die.

Voice Recognition

One very significant part of abiding in Christ and walking in freedom in our true identity is hearing God speak to us. Others ask me, "Jennifer, you talk a lot about God telling you things, giving you guidance and direction. How do you hear Him and how do you know it's Him talking to you? I don't feel like God talks to me." John 10:1-5 tells us about the sheep and the Good Shepherd and learning voice recognition.

"Truly, truly, I say to you, he who does not enter the sheepfold by the door but climbs in by another way, that man is a thief and a robber. But he who enters by the door is the shepherd of the sheep. To him the gatekeeper opens. The sheep hear his voice, and he calls his own sheep by name and leads them out. When he has brought out all his own, he goes before them, and the sheep follow him, for they know his voice. A stranger they will not follow, but they will flee from him, for they do not know the voice of strangers."

I ask, "When someone calls you on the phone, can you often tell who it is by their voice?" They answer, "Yes! I know the voice of *those I know well.*" It is the same with our Heavenly Father, the Good Shepherd. God is speaking all the time. We need to get to know Him so well that we recognize His voice, just like with a good friend. In developing an intimate relationship with the Lord, abiding in Him, we will be more tuned in and aware of when He is speaking to us, and how He speaks to us. After years of walking with the Lord and growing in an intimate relationship with Him I now easily recognize His voice versus lies from the enemy or my own thoughts. He speaks to me primarily through His Word, the Bible, pictures He gives me in my mind, thoughts/promptings, circumstances, through the Holy Spirit that lives in me and is the guardian of my spirit and soul, and sometimes through others or something I read.

For example, during my quiet times with the Lord or if I have a situation that I really need His guidance on, these are some steps I take to help me hear God's voice:

1. *Quiet myself down.* (Psalm 46:10) I find a comfortable place, unplug from technology, and stop all the "noise" that is constantly bombarding me. He often speaks through a still, quiet voice, and an inner witness to my Spirit. Sometimes I play quiet instrumental music. If I'm in the car, I turn off the radio.

2. *Pray and Read Scripture* (Psalm 143:8 & 10, Psalm 119:105) I will then PRAY and ask the Lord to speak to me, (Daniel 10:19) give me His wisdom, (Prov. 2:6) His mind (1 Corinthians 2:16) and understanding (1 John 5:20), and to lead me to any scripture that may speak to me in the situation. Sometimes He will direct me to read certain scripture, other times I am reading through a certain book of the Bible, and specific passages will minister to me. If I don't have my Bible with me I will ask the Lord to bring to my mind any scripture that will help me in the situation (thus, why it is also so important to KNOW the Word of God). He will remind me of His truth or insight, wisdom, understanding through the scripture and/or knowing His character. He will also speak to me through a devotional I read during my quiet time with Him, or another book I may be reading.

3. *Focus my thoughts on Jesus* (Psalm 145:5) I close my eyes and think about Jesus. I think about

His character, His love for me. I often picture myself with Him. Walking with Him, talking with Him, just being with Him. He often gives me pictures as I do this and it is usually a peaceful experience.

4. *Listen* (Habakkuk 2:1) I stay quiet and listen to what He is speaking to me through the Holy Spirit. I don't stop to analyze it or question it, I just go with the flow. I try to allow enough time to hear all He has to say to me.

5. *Write it down* (Habakkuk 2:2) I love to journal and write down scripture that speaks to me, what God is teaching me through it and what I hear Him saying to me. I write in all CAPS in my journal what I hear from God. Then it's easy for me to know when I go back to read my journal entries, what I wrote and what I heard God speak to me. I then test what I heard against God's Word and His character to know what is from Him and what is from my own analytical thinking. The more you do this the easier it will be to distinguish God's voice from your own or the enemy.

There are also times I am going about my day as usual and all of a sudden I will "hear" something in my head, or feel a very strong prompting about something, like, "Call so and so," "Get this for someone and take it to them," "Text your daughter with an encouraging word right now." When I am sure it is God speaking to me, I need to do what He asks trusting HE knows the purpose behind it, even if it seems silly or does not make sense. As I have followed through on these promptings I often find I am the answer to someone else's prayer or an encouragement at a time they most needed it.

Two-Way Communication

Another important part of having an intimate relationship with God and two-way communication is pouring out your heart to Him and asking Him questions. David did a lot of this in the Psalms! I do it all the time. I am often asking for ongoing guidance, wisdom, understanding, HELP! all throughout my day. I talk with Him as if He's sitting right there beside me. At times I don't hear anything or get a clear answer right away. In some situations I've had to wait, sometimes days or weeks, but if I don't hear anything or I have a "check in my spirit about something" (feel uneasy or lack of peace), I wait. God always brings an answer in HIS perfect timing. It is so easy to get ahead of God and operate in our own thinking and strength instead of going to Him and waiting on Him.

Our ministry board and event teams always begin our meetings with listening prayer. We go to God, the "coach" for the game plan *first* and ask Him to give us wisdom, His mind, unity, and to show us what His will is in a number of different circumstances or situations. Then we often are quiet and *listen* before sharing with one another what we feel God is telling us. It is really wonderful to see how it all fits together and we are unified in our sense of how He is leading us. When we go to Him *first* He guides our thinking, discussion and planning to be in line with His will, instead of planning and asking God to bless our plans!

When you are abiding and walking in a close, intimate relationship with the Lord you can be talking with Him and hearing from Him all throughout your day. HE has the plan for your life (Jeremiah 29:11). HE knows what your day is to be about and what His intentions are in it. Go to Him and ask Him what the plan is. You don't have to figure that out; you just need to be in close relationship with Him and follow the plan. It is so freeing to be in this type of relationship with the Lord. Remember *"the sheep know His voice."* Let HIM be your Good Shepherd, your life guide, the one who wants only the best for you and will not lead you astray or harm you.

It may take some time to learn to recognize and hear God speaking to you. But just like any good friendship, it will grow and deepen the more you spend time together. Remember, God wants to speak to you and for you to hear Him. Follow the suggested steps above to help yourself get started in listening and hearing from Him.

Walking In Our True Identity

Walking daily in our TRUE identity in Christ is difficult. In fact it is often impossible, and the harder we try to do it in our own strength, the more frustrated we will become. Jesus is the only One who has ever lived the perfect Christian life, and He is the only One who can live it today. The good news is He wants to live it through us! He has given us everything we need to walk a joyful, free, victorious life.

Take these steps to help you grow closer to Him and continue to abide and walk daily with Him in your TRUE Identity in Christ.

- **PRAISE AND WORSHIP GOD.** Keep your eyes focused on Him. It's difficult to stay sad and worried when you are singing or saying praises to God. The Bible tells us that *"Through Him then let us continually offer up a sacrifice of praise to God, that is, the fruit of lips that acknowledge His name"* (Hebrews 13:15). Put praise music on in the car as you drive to work or do housework at home. Peter started sinking as he walked toward Jesus on the water when he looked down at the waves lapping around his feet. When we are focused on our circumstances instead of our mighty, powerful, loving God, we will "sink." Don't focus on the enemy, focus on our Glorious God!

- **BE IN GOD'S WORD DAILY.** Keep saturating your mind with His TRUTH! (Remember the counterfeit money example?) John 8:31-32 tells us that if we ABIDE in His word, we are truly His disciples and we will know the TRUTH and the TRUTH will set us FREE. If we don't know the truth we will remain slaves to lies and bondage. Start each day with God's Word. Pray and ask Him how He wants to speak to you through His Word. The Bible is living and active (Hebrews 4:12), not a dead book with just words in it. There is a gold mine of truth and wisdom in how to handle any life situations you are facing right now and it will give you the power source to keep walking in freedom.

- **HAVE SOME QUIET TIME WITH THE LORD EVERY DAY.** Follow the steps to hearing God's voice as mentioned above. A key part of your quiet time is to be in God's Word every day. But it also can include reading a devotional, inspiring Christian book, singing, and should always include prayer. Commit your day to the Lord. Ask Him to guide you and lead you and give you wisdom in your actions, words, and choices. Ask Him to give you what you need to love and bless others in your day, to have HIS perspective on the situations you are in. Pray through putting the armor on. Visualize yourself doing it so you go out "Truthed" up and prayed up. You can pray and talk to God all day long, but it is often crucial to start our days with an intentional focus on the Lord. Even if you only have five minutes, start your day with Him.

- **KNOW THAT IT IS NOT A QUICK FIX AND NEEDS TO BE ONGOING PROCESS.** Be patient with God's timing, and know that you are in a war with Satan for your freedom. But know that God has already won the war and He will give you all you need to win each battle.

- **PUT YOUR SPIRITUAL ARMOR ON *EVERY DAY*.** Every soldier needs protection. Ephesians 6:11-18 describes every piece of armor we have been given in Christ. Note: you need to put the WHOLE armor on, not just part of it.

    o Belt of truth – (v 14)

    o Breastplate of righteousness (v 14) Protects your heart and vital organs o Shoes – the readiness given by the gospel of peace (v15)

o Shield of faith (v16) to deflect the fiery darts (lies) of the enemy

o Helmet of salvation (v17) Protects your mind

o Sword of the Spirit – The Word of God (v17) Cuts down any enemy with truth

o Prayer (v 18) Praying at all times in the Spirit. Holds all the armor together

Put it on, wear it, use it. Don't go out into battle naked and unprotected.

• **ERASE THE LIES WITH GOD'S TRUTH.** When Satan comes knocking on your door, remember to have Jesus answer it. Counter the lies with God's truth. Keep using the eraser of God's truth, and the lies that have caused deep wounds and hurts will be erased. Some find it helpful to stick scripture on their bathroom mirror, or have it in their car and purse. Memorize scriptural truths so you know them and are armed and ready to slash down and counter every lie.

• **BE CONFIDENT IN *WHO* AND *WHOSE* YOU ARE IN CHRIST, AND WHO HE IS *IN YOU*.** As Romans 8:37 tells us, *"We are more than conquerors through Him who loved us."* As we remind ourselves of our standing in Christ and who He is in us, we will have more confidence in being ourselves, being real, being free. He has given us everything we need by putting His Spirit in us for us to walk daily in victory and freedom. Believe it!

• **BIBLE STUDY, SMALL GROUP, FELLOWSHIP GROUP, ACCOUNTABILITY PARTNER.** Get into a regular Bible study. This is a wonderful way to learn more about God's Word, grow in your faith and trust in Him. Join a small group or fellowship group, and have an accountability partner. We were not meant to walk this path alone. We need to build one another's faith, encourage one another, pray for one another, and help one another walk in our true identity.

• **HAVE AN UPWARD AND OUTWARD FOCUS.** Chin up! Keep your eyes focused upward on the Lord. Look to Him in all things. He will set you free from yourself and you will be available to serve Him. God tells us in 1 Corinthians 12:7 that each of us is given a gift of the Spirit for the common good. To build up the Body of Christ. Pray and ask the Lord to show you how He has gifted you. "God does not call the equipped, He equips the called." Use the gifts He gives you and serve in your church, ministry, and community. Be His hands and feet to a lost and hurting world. You will be blessed as you bless others.

Here is also a "Walking in Your True Identity Checklist" my friend Debbie Jones put together.

Walking In Your True Identity Checklist

✔ Acknowledge your feelings and your situation. Take your complaint to the Lord.

✔ Listen to God

✔ Meditate on His Truth in His Word every day

✔ Praise and thanksgiving – Philippians 4:8

✔ Watch what you put into your mind or what you allow to stay there (2 Corinthians 10:5)

✔ Guard your heart remembering that what goes into your heart comes out of your mouth (Matthew 15:16-20, Psalm 41:6, Proverbs 18:21)

✔ Words have power, use them wisely (Proverbs 15:4, James 3:5-6, 8-9)

✔ Get wisdom and understanding before you act, like Jesus did before He cleansed the temple.

✔ Confess and repent

✔ Forgive

✔ Take authority over the enemy, use the keys Jesus gave us (Matthew 16:19, Luke 10:19)

✔ Put on the whole armor of God each day (Ephesians 6:10-20)

✔ Step out in faith in what God is telling and leading you to do

Help For The Journey

Look at some of the resources in the back of this book. Use them as tools to help you learn more about your personality type, work through the process of identifying lies, renouncing them, countering them with truth, and embracing your TRUE identity in Christ.

Periodically you may need to go back and review some of the principles laid out in this book. There may be times when certain issues resurface, and it might be helpful to address them in light of some of the Biblical truths found in this book.

Remember that God has given us EVERYTHING we need to walk in freedom and victory. Be encouraged by these words in Hebrews 12:1-2, *"Therefore, since we are surrounded by so great a cloud of witnesses, let us also lay aside every weight, and sin which clings so closely, and let us run with endurance the race that is set before us, looking to Jesus, the founder and perfector of our faith, who for the joy that was set before Him endured the cross, despising the shame, and is seated at the right hand of the throne of God."*

Becoming more confident in your TRUE identity and daily walking in it takes time. Whenever you feel the enemy creeping back in to drag you down and chip away at the confidence, remember all the Lord has taught you and helped you with in reading through this book and His Word. Come back to this—the TRUTH, and remind yourself that you are a WARRIOR PRINCESS WITHOUT FEAR! A PRECIOUS, BEAUTIFUL DAUGHTER OF THE KING!

REMEMBER:

> REALIZE – How God "wired" and made you
>
> REFLECT – See yourself in God's mirror as HE sees you
>
> RECOGNIZE – The lies you have been believing
>
> REPENT – Of the thoughts and behavior the lies led to, be forgiven through salvation in Christ.
>
> RENOUNCE – The lies
>
> REPLACE – The lies with God's TRUTH
>
> RENEW – Be transformed by the renewing of your mind
>
> RESTORE – Restore relationships through forgiveness
>
> RELEASED – To be all God intended you to be
>
> RESULT – You are a NEW CREATION in Christ (As one who has surrendered to and accepted Christ as Savior and Lord)—FREE in your TRUE Identity
>
> REJOICE – You are a DAUGHTER of the KING!

From Ugly Ducklings to Swans. From Bondage to Freedom. From Inward Focus to Upward and Outward Focus —Open vessels to do God's Kingdom work.

Before You Read On

1. Are you "winding up" each morning, or "plugging in" to the power source?

2. What steps can you take to move from "striving" to "abiding?"

3. Do you hear God speaking to you? If not, what steps can you take to become more familiar with the Shepherd's voice and hear Him more clearly? How does He speak to you?

4. Who is your guide? Are there areas in your life you need to trust the Lord, instead of the world, to guide you through?

5. Are there steps listed in the "Walking in Your True Identity Checklist" you feel you need improvement in? What can you do now to begin incorporating them into your daily or weekly routine?

6. Review this chapter frequently to take your "spiritual temperature" and be encouraged in ways to stay connected and deepen your relationship with Christ, allowing you to experience more freedom in your true identity in Him!

7. Remember WHO and WHOSE you truly are, how much God loves and cherishes you, and that you are never alone.

SUGGESTED PRAYER

Father,
help me to take off my mask.
Help me to slip my hand in Yours
and yield the parts of myself I've protected so carefully.
Thank you that I don't have to be anyone
but who You created me to be.
Help me discover who that is.
I give you access, Holy Spirit.
Show me my TRUE IDENTITY—
all that I am in You.
Give me the courage to change those things
that keep me from being real.
Thank you that You accept me as I am
and that You will never leave me.
Help me every day, Lord, to become
more of the authentic,
beautiful woman You created me to be.
I eagerly look forward to walking in
my TRUE IDENTITY
and living as a
Daughter of the King!
In Jesus' Name ~ Amen

❀ ❀ ❀

Before You Close This Book

I know why God's timing to write this book is now. I wasn't ready twenty years ago. I was not completely free of the lies and bondages. I was still carrying my "backpack" around, convinced there was no way to get it off. I needed to experience more of God's transforming power and healing in me and come to a place of confidence in WHO and WHOSE I was in Him, and who He truly is IN ME. I needed to spend many more years saturated in His Word learning to recognize the lies when they popped into my mind, and counter them with His truth. I needed to learn how to trust God more to step outside my comfort zones and do new things for Him I never imagined I could do. And finally I could break the chains that held me in bondages and be set FREE to be all the King had planned and desired for me to be.

Indeed there was a princess born that cold, blustery December morning. She was transformed from an ugly duckling into a beautiful, sanctified swan. HIS swan. HIS PRINCESS! And at last SHE knew it!

Just a few months ago, God gave me this poem one morning during my quiet time with Him.

Treasured Swan

My life was on a lonely path
So full of hurt and taunting laughs
I longed for love, to be embraced
Accepted into a special place
But all I heard was you're not enough
You're damaged goods, unsightly stuff

I hated life, hated myself
Always felt like I was put on a shelf
Wanted to change the playground rules
Only the cute and talented reign at school
The different, unusual, don't belong
They're bullied, teased, and always wrong

I wanted out from this tortured place
So sick of being teased about my face
The models on the magazines
Their perfect smiles always mocking me
Striving for something I could never be
Escaping the pain was all I could see

But You came and rescued this shattered soul
Lovingly mended life's burdensome toll
You changed me from the inside out
You gave me hope, drove out all doubt
Gave me strength to carry on
Showed me I was your treasured swan

Because you died on Calvary
My sins are cleansed, the captive free
You showed me my TRUE identity
Beautiful daughter, precious, and loved
Kissed by my Heavenly Father from above
Free to be all you designed me to be
In your loving arms for eternity.

I often have a picture in my mind of a vast canyon, like the Grand Canyon in Arizona, with a huge, wooden cross, spanned across it. Jesus is on one side and there are hundreds of women on the other. God showed me instead of standing on the one side with Jesus, calling out to the women on the other side to come across, I needed to go across myself and walk back with them and place their hand in Jesus' hand. I begin to run across to the side where all the women are, and one by one, bring them back across to Jesus. I place their hand in His and He hugs them, and crowns them, and sings praises over them. As more women are brought across and are together with Jesus, they are dancing and singing, having a grand celebration with God.

That picture is this book. It is my hope that as I have "come across the canyon," and been able to walk with you back across and put your hand firmly in Jesus' hand. That you will be set free in your TRUE Identity as His precious daughter and join the celebration with God!

Thank you for taking this journey with me. Keep your "backpack" off and go dancing with God! May He abundantly bless you as you walk daily with Him.

"I have no greater joy than to hear that my children are walking in truth." 3 John 1:4

Resources

Lies
Lies Progression Chart
Lies We Believe list

True Identity
In the Mirror of God's Word

Daughter Of The King
Mirror Drawing Page

Personalities
The Four Temperaments
Personality Circle

Breaking The Chains
Lies We Believe with Scripture to Counter
Belief Systems Chart

Lies Progression Chart

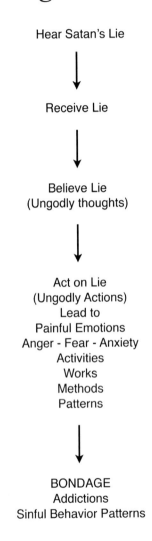

Hear Satan's Lie

Receive Lie

Believe Lie
(Ungodly thoughts)

Act on Lie
(Ungodly Actions)
Lead to
Painful Emotions
Anger - Fear - Anxiety
Activities
Works
Methods
Patterns

BONDAGE
Addictions
Sinful Behavior Patterns

Lies We Believe

- ☐ GOD IS NOT REALLY GOOD
- ☐ GOD DOESN'T LOVE ME
- ☐ GOD IS JUST LIKE MY FATHER
- ☐ GOD IS NOT REALLY ENOUGH
- ☐ I'M NOT WORTH ANYTHING
- ☐ I NEED TO LEARN TO LOVE MYSELF
- ☐ I CAN'T HELP THE WAY I AM
- ☐ I HAVE MY RIGHTS
- ☐ PHYSICAL BEAUTY MATTERS MORE THAN INNER BEAUTY
- ☐ I AM A LOSER, I CAN'T DO ANYTHING RIGHT
- ☐ I CAN SIN AND GET AWAY WITH IT
- ☐ I'M NOT ANY DIFFERENT THAN I WAS BEFORE I BECAME A CHRISTIAN
- ☐ GOD CAN'T FORGIVE WHAT I'VE DONE
- ☐ NO ONE EVER CHOOSES ME
- ☐ I CANNOT WALK IN CONSISTENT VICTORY OVER SIN
- ☐ I WISH I WERE TALENTED LIKE SHE IS
- ☐ I CAN MAKE IT WITHOUT CONSISTENT TIME IN THE WORD AND PRAYER
- ☐ I MUST HAVE THE APPROVAL OF OTHERS TO FEEL GOOD ABOUT MYSELF
- ☐ I HAVE TO HAVE A HUSBAND TO BE HAPPY
- ☐ IT IS MY RESPONSIBILITY TO CHANGE MY MATE
- ☐ I CAN'T FORGIVE MYSELF
- ☐ MY LIFE HAS NO PURPOSE OR DIRECTION
- ☐ I COULD NEVER GO TO HEAVEN
- ☐ IF I FEEL SOMETHING IT MUST BE TRUE
- ☐ I CAN'T CONTROL MY EMOTIONS
- ☐ IF GOD LOVES ME, HOW COULD HE LET THIS HAPPEN?
- ☐ I WOULD BE HAPPY IF _____
- ☐ I AM ALL ALONE AND FEEL SO EMPTY INSIDE
- ☐ MY FINANCIAL SITUATION IS HOPELESS
- ☐ I JUST CAN'T TAKE ANY MORE
- ☐ I AM ALL SUFFICIENT/I DON'T NEED ANYONE
- ☐ EVERYONE IS AGAINST ME
- ☐ I CAN'T FORGIVE THE PERSON WHO HURT ME

True Identity

Therefore, if anyone is in Christ, he is a new creation... 2 Cor. 5:17

In the Mirror of God's Word, I See...

1 Samuel 12:22	I am His own.
1 Samuel 16:7	He sees my heart.
2 Kings 20:5	He heals me.
1 Chron. 28:8	I will pass on an inheritance.
Job 23:10	He knows the way that I take.
Psalm 16:11	He gives me eternal pleasures at His right hand.
Psalm 21:6	He makes me glad with the joy of His presence.
Psalm 27:4	I will gaze upon the beauty of the Lord forever.
Psalm 27:10	He will never forsake me.
Psalm 34:18	He is near me.
Psalm 45:11	He is enthralled by my beauty.
Psalm 91:14	He rescues me.
Psalm 103:4	He crowns me with love and compassion.
Psalm 107:9	He satisfies my hunger with good things.
Psalm 139:14	I am wonderfully made.
Proverbs 12:25	He cheers my heart.
Proverbs 15:4	I speak words of life to others.
Isaiah 41:18	He makes my wilderness like Eden.
Isaiah 53:4	He bears my pain.
Isaiah 61:3	He gives me a crown of beauty instead of ashes.
Isaiah 61:10	He wraps me in a robe of righteousness.
Isaiah 62:2	He calls me by a new name.
Isaiah 64:8	I am His workmanship.
Jeremiah 1:5	He knows me.
Jeremiah 14:9	I bear His name.
Jeremiah 31:3	He loves me with an everlasting love.
Mark 6:31	He takes me to a quiet place and gives me rest.
John 7:24	He does not judge me by appearances.
John 8:36	He sets me free.
Romans 15:7	I am accepted in the Beloved.
2 Cor. 3:16	He sees me as I am.
2 Cor. 4:17	He turns my hardship to glory.
Galatians 5:1	He delivers me.
Ephesians 1:3	He blesses me with every spiritual blessing.
Philippians 3:13	He redeems my past.
2 Thes. 2:16	He gives me hope.
2 Peter 1:3	He gives me everything I need.

True Identity Ministries, Inc. 2011-2013   www.TrueIdentityMinistries.org

Daughter of the King
Mirror Drawing Page

Personalitites
The Four Temperaments

S
THE FUN WAY

Strengths	Weaknesses
Optimistic	Compulsive
Sense of humor	Naive
Cheerful	Undisciplined
Creative & Colorful	Easily distracted
Inspiring	Doesn't listen
Makes friends easily	Overly talkative

Needs	Basic Desire
Attention	Have FUN
Approval	
Affection	
Acceptance	

C
MY WAY

Strengths	Weaknesses
Born leader	Bossy
Dynamic & active	Impatient
Decisive	Inflexible
Organizes well	Manipulative
Undaunted	Demanding
Excels in emergencies	Dominating

Needs	Basic Desire
Achievement	Have CONTROL
Admiration	

P
THE EASY WAY

Strengths	Weaknesses
Easy-going	Unenthusiastic
Sympathetic	Indecisive
Patient	Fearful
Steady	Lazy
Agreeable	Passive
Good listener	Uninvolved

Needs	Basic Desire
Sense of worth	Have PEACE
Respect	
No confrontation	

M
THE RIGHT WAY

Strengths	Weaknesses
Thoughtful	Moody
Artistic	Low self-image
Sensitive	Introspective
Perfectionist	Hard to please
Neat & tidy	Withdrawn
Faithful & devoted	Critical

Needs	Basic Desire
Support	Have PERFECTION
Order	
Sensitivity	
Space	

Adapted from *Personality Plus* by Florence Littaeur

Personalities
Personality Circle

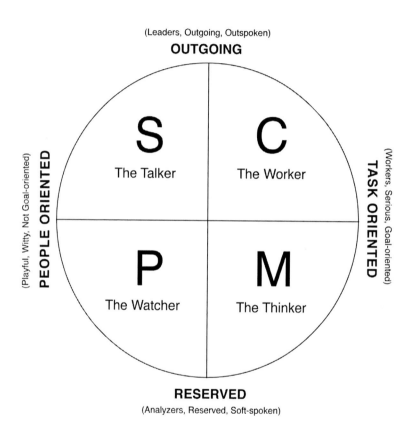

Breaking the Chains
Lies We Believe
with Scripture truth to counter

LIES:

SCRIPTURAL TRUTH TO COUNTER:

LIES	SCRIPTURAL TRUTH TO COUNTER
☐ GOD IS NOT REALLY GOOD	☐ Psalm 119:68
☐ GOD DOESN'T LOVE ME	☐ Romans. 5:8, John 3:16, 1 John 3:1, Ephesians 3:17-19
☐ GOD IS JUST LIKE MY FATHER	☐ Hebrews 1:3, Hebrews 12:10
☐ GOD IS NOT REALLY ENOUGH	☐ John 10:10, Colossians 2:10
☐ I'M NOT WORTH ANYTHING	☐ Deuteronomy 14:2, Ephesians 2:10
☐ I NEED TO LEARN TO LOVE MYSELF	☐ Luke 9:23
☐ I CAN'T HELP THE WAY I AM	☐ Romans 6:6
☐ I HAVE MY RIGHTS	☐ Jonah 4
☐ PHYSICAL BEAUTY MATTERS MORE THAN INNER BEAUTY	☐ 1 Samuel 16:7, Proverbs 31:30
☐ I AM A LOSER, I CAN'T DO ANYTHING RIGHT	☐ Philippians 4:13, Colossians 2:9-10
☐ I CAN SIN AND GET AWAY WITH IT	☐ John 8:34, Romans 6:23
☐ I'M NO DIFFERENT THAN BEFORE I BECAME A CHRISTIAN	☐ 2 Corinthians 5:17
☐ GOD CAN'T FORGIVE WHAT I'VE DONE	☐ 1 John 1:9
☐ NO ONE EVER CHOOSES ME	☐ John 15:16
☐ I CANNOT WALK IN CONSISTENT VICTORY OVER SIN	☐ James 4:7, 1 John 5:4-5
☐ I WISH I WERE TALENTED LIKE SHE IS	☐ Romans 12:6
☐ I CAN MAKE IT WITHOUT CONSISTENT TIME IN THE WORD AND PRAYER	☐ John 15:4
☐ I MUST HAVE OTHERS' APPROVAL TO FEEL GOOD ABOUT MYSELF	☐ Galatians 1:10
☐ I HAVE TO HAVE A HUSBAND TO BE HAPPY	☐ Revelation 21:9
☐ IT IS MY RESPONSIBILITY TO CHANGE MY MATE	☐ Matthew 7:1-3
☐ I CAN'T FORGIVE MYSELF	☐ Romans 8:1
☐ MY LIFE HAS NO PURPOSE OR DIRECTION	☐ Jeremiah 29:11
☐ I COULD NEVER GO TO HEAVEN	☐ Ephesians 2:8-9
☐ IF I FEEL SOMETHING IT MUST BE TRUE	☐ John 8:31-32
☐ I CAN'T CONTROL MY EMOTIONS	☐ Romans 6:6, 2 Corinthians 10:5
☐ IF GOD LOVES ME, HOW COULD HE LET THIS HAPPEN?	☐ Romans 8:28
☐ I WOULD BE HAPPY IF _____	☐ Psalm 126:3, Philippians 4:11, 1 Thessalonians 5:18
☐ I AM ALL ALONE AND FEEL SO EMPTY INSIDE	☐ Colossians 2:10, Hebrews 13:5
☐ MY FINANCIAL SITUATION IS HOPELESS	☐ Philippians 4:19
☐ I JUST CAN'T TAKE ANY MORE	☐ Romans 8:37
☐ I AM ALL SUFFICIENT / I DON'T NEED ANYONE	☐ 2 Corinthians 3:5-6
☐ EVERYONE IS AGAINST ME	☐ Romans 8:31
☐ I CAN'T FORGIVE THE PERSON WHO HURT ME	☐ Ephesians 4:32

Breaking the Chains
Belief Systems Chart I

Satan's Lie Your worth = Your performance plus other's opinions	Consequences of believing Satan's lies	God's Truth Your worth = What God says about you	Results of believing God's Truth
I must meet certain standards in order to feel good about myself	Because I fear failure: • I want to be perfect • I am too concerned about my success • I withdraw from risks • I have to win • I manipulate others for my benefit	I am completely forgiven by God, fully pleasing to Him, and no longer have to fear failure. Romans 3:19-25 II Cor. 5:21	Because I am in Christ: • I am free from the fear of failure • I seek the right things through Him • I have a growing love for Him • I can serve others with His love
I must have the approval of others to feel good about myself	Because I fear rejection: • I try to please others at any costs • I am too sensitive to criticism • I withdraw to avoid disapproval • I fear being open and vulnerable	I am totally accepted by God and do not have to fear rejection. Col 1: 19-22	Because I am in Christ: • I am free from the fear of rejection • I can be open and vulnerable • I can relax with others • I can receive criticism
When I fail, I feel I am unworthy of love and deserve to be punished.	Because I fear punishment: • I don't forgive others when they fail • I blame others when I fail • I feel far away from God	I am deeply loved by God, do not have to fear punishment, and do not need to punish others when they fail. I John 4: 9-10	Because I am in Christ: • I am free from the fear of punishment • I can forgive as Christ forgave me • I can feel deeply loved by Him
I am what I am. I cannot change. I am hopeless.	Because I fear shame: • I feel inferior • I often feel hopeless • I am destructive toward myself and others	I have been made brand new, am complete in Him, and need not feel any shame. II Cor. 5:17	Because I am in Christ: • I am free from shame • I have Christ centered confidence • I have His hope, courage, and peace

We can renew our minds by using our emotions to analyze our belief system.

Neil Anderson

Breaking the Chains
Belief Systems Chart II

We can renew our minds by using our emotions to analyze our belief system.

SITUATION

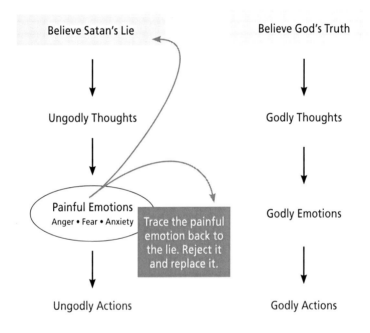

Believe Satan's Lie

Ungodly Thoughts

Painful Emotions
Anger • Fear • Anxiety

Trace the painful emotion back to the lie. Reject it and replace it.

Ungodly Actions

Believe God's Truth

Godly Thoughts

Godly Emotions

Godly Actions

Neil Anderson

Notes

Chapter 3: The Ugly Duckling

Hans Christian Anderson, *The Ugly Duckling*, 1843.

Chapter 4: Lies, Lies, Lies

Sarah Young, *Jesus Calling* (Nashville, TN: Thomas Nelson, 2004), February 12.

Nancy Leigh DeMoss, *Lies Women Believe* (Chicago, IL: Moody Press, 2001), p. 32.

Chapter 5: Smorgasbord of Lies

Sarah Young, *Jesus Calling* (Nashville, TN: Thomas Nelson, 2004), February 28.

Chapter 6: Weighed Down With Lies

Boyd Bailey, *Wisdom Hunters Devotionals: Demolish Strongholds,* (Roswell, GA: Wisdom Hunters, 2012), February 27. www.WisdomHunters.com

Chapter 7: Mistaken Identity

Nancy Leigh DeMoss, *Lies Women Believe* (Chicago, IL: Moody Press, 2001), p. 66.

Chapter 8: Breaking the Chains

Neil T. Anderson, The Steps to Freedom in Christ (Ventura, CA: Gospel Light Publishing, 1990), p. 4.

Chapter 9: Throwing Off the Backpack

For a fuller study of freedom in Christ see Neil T. Anderson, *Victory Over the Darkness* (Ventura, CA: Regal Books from Gospel Light Publishing, 1990).

Neil T. Anderson, *Stomping Out the Darkness* (Ventura, CA: Regal Books from Gospel Light Publishing, 1993), p. 73.

By de Fabrique, Nathalie; Romano, Stephen J.; Vecchi, Gregory M.; van Hasselt, Vincent B. *"Understanding the Stockholm Syndrome."* FBI Law Enforcement Bulletin. July 2007.
http://www.fbi.gov/stats-services/publications/law-enforcement-bulletin/2007-pdfs/july07leb.pdf

Chapter 10: The Lock on the Chains

For a fuller study on forgiveness see Bruce and Toni Hebel, *Forgiving Forward: Unleashing the Forgiveness Revolution* (Fayetteville, GA, 2011).

Chapter 11: True Identity

Sharon Jaynes, *The Ultimate Makeover* (Chicago, IL: Moody Publishers, 2003), p. 79

Chapter 12: Uniquely You

For a fuller study on personality types see Florence Littauer, *Personality Plus* (Grand Rapids, MI: Revell Publishing, 1983).

For a fuller study on personality types see Marita Littauer, *Wired That Way* (Ventura, CA: Regal Books from Gospel Light Publishing, 2006).

Chapter 13: Daughter of the King

Henri J. M. Nouwen, *Here and Now: Living in the Spirit* (New York, NY: Crossroad Publishing Company, 1994) p. 134-135

John and Staci Eldredge, *Captivating* (Nashville, TN: Thomas Nelson, 2004), p. 135

The Father's Love Letter used by permission Father Heart Communications © 1999-2011
www.FathersLoveLetter.com

Chapter 14: Embracing Your True Identity

John Piper, *Christian Hedonism*, 1995 © 2012 Desiring God Foundation. www.desiringGod.org.

Chapter 15: Walking In Your True Identity

For a fuller study on how to hear God's voice see Mark and Patti Virkler, *4 Keys to Hearing God's Voice* (Shippensburg, PA: Destiny Image ® Publishers, Inc., 2010).

What you are is God's gift to you,
what you become is your gift to God.

~ Hans Urs von Balthasar, *Prayer*

About the Author
Jennifer Brommet

Jennifer hails from Wisconsin and has a background in advertising and graphic design. She worked for the Billy Graham Evangelistic Association (BGEA) as Art Director in Minneapolis, Minnesota, and Production Coordinator for the 1986 BGEA International Conference for Itinerant Evangelists in Amsterdam, the Netherlands. While living in Amsterdam, she met and married her husband, Remco.

God prepared Jennifer for the call to start and lead True Identity Ministries through her own personal journey from severe rejection and depression as a child and young adult to freedom in understanding and embracing her TRUE Identity in Christ. She has a deep passion for others to understand how much God loves them, know His Word of truth, deepen their relationship with Him, and be set free to be all He designed and desires for them to be.

Jennifer has over twenty-five years of experience in women's ministry which has included; organizing and leading women's retreats and events, leading women's Bible study groups and small groups, teaching and speaking, marriage ministry with her husband, and serving as the Women's Ministry Director at her church in California, before moving to Georgia in 2007 and founding True Identity Ministries in 2008. She also has over twenty years of administrative and event planning experience.

Jennifer loves seeing God's beautiful creation through a camera lens and capturing life's special moments digitally. She also enjoys expressing herself creatively through drawing, sewing, decorating and design. She loves to travel, see new places and meet new people. She likes to exercise and go for vigorous walks with her husband, and when she has some quiet moments, she loves to read and journal.

Jennifer and Remco live in Cumming, Georgia and have two grown daughters. Carina is pursuing a master's in screenwriting in London and Sophia will be starting college in the fall of 2013.

About
True Identity Ministries

God's message of embracing your true identity is universal and life-transforming. True Identity Ministries is a nondenominational nonprofit ministry with a board of directors, prayer support team, advisory committee, and a wonderful group of volunteers.

Our goal is to help others from all walks of life be set free from lies and deception, be awakened to the truth of being all God desires and purposed for them to be, and apply that to their daily lives.

Internationally, True Identity is a ministry partner with Divine Providence Training Center for pastors in Kenya, has established a Kenyan office with a full-time director, and has 25 certified Kenyan instructors. Opportunities for workshops and retreats continue to expand in Africa and in South America with interest emerging in Eastern Europe and southeast Asia.

Contact Jennifer Brommet to schedule a True Identity event with your church group, ministry, and/or ministry leadership team.

Jennifer and Remco Brommet are available to speak at events, retreats, and conferences.

info@TrueIdentityMinistries.org
www.TrueIdentityMinistries.org

True Identity Ministries is a 501(c)3 nonprofit ministry. All donations are tax deductible.

Thank you for reading
True Identity.

Find out more at
www.TrueIdentityMinistries.org.